EDINBURGH
THE
NEW TOWN

For Struan
so that he will never forget his
happy school days in the New Town.

EDINBURGH
THE
NEW TOWN

IAN NIMMO

JOHN DONALD PUBLISHERS

EDINBURGH

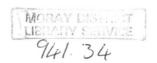
ISBN 0 85976 323 4

A catalogue record for this book
is available from the British Library.

Typeset by Pioneer Associates, Perthshire
Printed and bound in Great Britain by
Courier International, East Kilbride

ACKNOWLEDGEMENTS

During the research and writing of this book I have received many kindnesses and help from Edinburgh citizens of all ranks. I would therefore like to thank: the staffs of the National Library of Scotland and Edinburgh Central Library; The Scotsman Publications for permission to use their photographs and in particular Mr Bill Brady and the library staff; the Edinburgh New Town Conservation Committee; the Cockburn Association, the Edinburgh Civic Trust; The National Galleries of Scotland; The National Trust for Scotland; The Royal Commission on the Ancient and Historic Monuments of Scotland; Edinburgh District Council for all their ready help; Hurd, Rowland Partnership; Lothians and Borders Police, with a special thank you to the Gayfield Square force and particularly to Chief Inspector Douglas Mowat, now promoted to Police Headquarters in Fettes Avenue, and to Norma Graham, now Detective Sergeant; staff and pupils at Broughton High School, The Edinburgh Academy, Fettes College; Lady Dunpark, Hamish Coghill, John C. Hope, Alisdair Hunter, Dr David and Wendy Munro, Hugh Macdougall, Jim McKay, Gwen Rayner, W. Gordon Smith, Professor Alan Thomson, John Tuckwell, the members of my reminiscence group, Margaret Gibson, Susan Imrie, Jessie Nolan, John Kirk, Colin Paterson and Ian Paterson. I am indebted to Mrs Johnson for permission to use the photographs taken by her late husband, J. Johnson. My gratitude to Edinburgh writers past and present who have touched on the New Town in books and newspaper articles in *The Scotsman* and *Evening News* and to those many people who helped me with information, advice and encouragement. Thank you.

Elsewhere in this book I have referred to those celebrities who have passed across the Edinburgh stage through the centuries and also to some who follow in their footsteps today. Even in the few months it has taken to write this book the speed of change is altering circumstances. People are changing jobs, retiring, moving to different areas, dying. I therefore hope those named in this book and affected by that inevitable process of change will forgive me in the few instances where I have been unable to keep pace while this book has been in production.

CONTENTS

INTRODUCTION

BACK TO THE FUTURE

'I BELIEVE when a man loses contact with the past he loses his soul. Likewise if we deny the architectural past — and the lessons to be learned from our ancestors — then our buildings also lose their souls.'

HRH THE PRINCE OF WALES

ALTHOUGH Prince Charles may never appreciate Scotland's capital to the same degree as the majority of its citizens, he is nonetheless familiar enough with Edinburgh to compare it with other cities, proclaim its virtues and declare it his favourite.

What The Prince of Wales likes about Edinburgh is its sense of history, its classical good looks, the planning excellence of the two-centuries-old New Town, its fastidious, disciplined harmony of style, the bright green of the Edinburgh environment, the large residential community enjoying a high quality of life at the very heart of town, while many other cities have become night-time deserts devoid of people. All these factors appeal to Prince Charles's perception of city 'rightness'.

The environment generally, and how it is treated, is obviously something the Prince feels deeply about. In this respect, he has not been backward in telling people what he believes, and architects and planners more than most have sometimes received the critical edge of his comments. He believes there has been a movement away from the past into dreariness, heartlessness, ugliness and mediocrity, to use his words. Too many architects have allowed themselves to be dictated to by fashion and fads. The rule books have been thrown out of the window for experimentation which has resulted in the creation of monsters.

1

This aerial view of St Andrew Square shows Sir Laurence Dundas's town house in the foreground in front of the dome with the small garden leading to the Square. It was from here the whole of the New Town was surveyed and a plaque on the floor at the entrance to the Royal Bank of Scotland now marks the starting point. At the other end of George Street the green fields around what was to be Charlotte Square were daily yielding the workmen a healthy diet of snared rabbits and hares and, occasionally, one of the Earl of Moray's pheasants.

People's interests have been set aside too easily and they have had little say in the matter. The public have accepted what they were given, and too often it was not what they wanted.

Some architects have responded in kind and bluntly suggested to the Prince that he should mind his own business and stick to subjects he knows something

2

New Town fanlights come in a variety of designs, but these twins seen in Northumberland Street are typical and attractive. Northumberland Street has weathered the years well, but the impingement of the motor car, as on other central streets, harasses it sorely. Every available foot of space has been given over to the car. The two rear lanes, where the old stables and carriage sheds were sited, are mostly garages and even some of the gardens have been squeezed to accommodate a vehicle.

about. Others, more thoughtfully, have considered and recognised the home truths in the Prince's arguments. They have also noted the weight of public support behind them and positively joined in the debate, which is no more than Prince Charles has been seeking.

The fact is, of course, that the environment today is everyone's business.

What is happening to the air we breathe, the pollution of rivers and seas, the threat to wild life, the destruction of tropical forest, the obliteration of heritage, the herding of people into instant ghettos, the violence of inner cities, the

Elegant style was everything to the Georgians; although there was scope for variation it was critical that there should be general uniformity to the theme. This four-panel door in St Bernard's Crescent is a variation to the normal six panels and it would not be to everyone's taste to highlight the panels in paint. But nowadays residents take enormous pride in their historic homes and conform as far as possible to the guidelines, which include suggested colour schemes. The development was by James Milne and completed in 1824.

disposal of toxic material, the rise and rise of junk architecture, the rain that falls as acid, the whole range of environmental issues across the world are now matters of urgent concern to people. Firmly and properly they have been elevated to the public arena for discussion. Close to home, among other matters, that environment agenda also includes the conservation and sensitive development of beautiful, historical city centres like the Old Town and New Town of Edinburgh.

Prince Charles is one of the most influential figures to demonstrate concern about environment and conservation issues. It is therefore easily understood why he so approves of the professional and dedicated manner in which the Edinburgh conservation associations in the centre of town go about their business like zealots. Along with most other people he also admires how those early planners used Edinburgh's natural terrain to best advantage, and their sense and use of space remains obviously masterly. Some of the outstanding restoration work has given him enormous satisfaction and the planning symmetry and Georgian elegance of the New Town have always delighted him. These are indeed the handsome and civilised central oases of tradition and splendour of Edinburgh. They lend the city its style and grace and perhaps even its character, for the moving of a lamp-post, the colour of a door or drainpipe or shop front, paving stones and windows, railings and astragals are matters that must be closely scrutinised in case somehow they clash with the overall harmony of relationships. The result, at least in the eyes of Prince Charles, is the most beautiful city in Britain.

It would be reassuring to believe that the historical and aesthetic good looks of central Edinburgh would be respected without the need for a pack of watchdogs, but the world at large remains insensitive, even hostile to delicate flowers, and without the vigilance of such organisations as the Cockburn Association and the New Town Conservation Committee, marauding speculators, well-meaning but ill-informed companies and the wear and tear of Edinburgh's vicious climate over the centuries would leave the city looking substantially different, less attractive and certainly with a major loss of heritage.

There are other parts of Edinburgh less pleasing, of course, and perhaps less familiar to Prince Charles. That New Town abomination in concrete called the St James Centre, for example, with the fifth-rate New St Andrew's House rising like Castle Dreich behind it, is unworthy of Scotland's capital. In Prince Charles's list of British architectural carbuncles (his expression again) it would sit easily. At least the Secretary of State for Scotland has preserved the dignity of his office by removing himself and colleagues back to old St Andrew's House, which remains one of the more interesting Edinburgh survivors of the 1930s. Perhaps the main value of the St James Centre today is to act as a reminder that we do not wish to see its like again. Regrettably, lack of conservation policy and commitment

Looking down on Moray Place, one of the jewels of the New Town and the work of architect Gillespie Graham. His masterpiece was so magnificent that it moved the emphasis of fashionable Edinburgh westwards away from the less successful Calton Hill development. Part of the plan was the creation of landscaped "Pleasure Grounds" on the ravine above the Water of Leith, which remain in place. At the bottom right of the picture is the classical St Bernard's Well built over a mineral spring in 1789.

OPPOSITE

It is not just the harmony of the buildings that makes the New Town special. The same creative attention to detail was taken inside and out of sight to create a complete effect. Some of the Georgian ceilings and chimney pieces are still in place as works of art. They were normally of marble or polished slate and it has been known for thieves nowadays to leave contents but make off with the fireplace. This interior from Great King Street gives an indication of Georgian style. Invariably the dining room was on ground floor level, the drawing room on the first floor and the kitchen in the basement.

An atmospheric corner of Edinburgh at the rear of Dundas House, now the Royal Bank of Scotland, which faces on to St Andrew Square. This little street is Register Place, near Register House, and in the old days it was a busy part of town with the densely-populated St James Square behind and the Cafe Royal close by. As darkness fell it was a place of shadows and lurking figures came over from the Old Town on thieving missions with an easy escape route back into the myriad closes and side streets across and below North Bridge.

in the past resulted in the original attractive Georgian St James Square being razed when it might have been saved.

When Prince Charles talks of Edinburgh delights clearly he does not mean West Pilton or Muirhouse or Niddrie or West Granton or Wester Hailes or Craigmillar and other well-intentioned housing schemes that were failures even before the tenants moved in and later no matter how hard people tried to

The panorama of the Calton Hill with its collection of monuments, the flank of Arthur's Seat on the right, the Forth estuary in the background and the city spread all around. In the old days jousts took place in the valley in the foreground and the Carmelite Monastery of Greenside once stood there, where burnings for heresy and witchcraft took place. It later became a leper colony and gallows were erected to give quick dispatch to anyone who stepped outside its walls. The Quarry Holes were at the other side of the hill and favoured as a place for duels. Perhaps the biggest crime perpetrated in the area was the building of the cheapskate concrete monstrosities of New St Andrew's House in the foreground and the St James Centre. Viewed from the Calton Hill they stick in the eye as a most regrettable New Town intrusion.

overcome. No doubt he is well aware of that 'other' Edinburgh outside the tourist trail because he has seen it reflected throughout Britain as well as Europe.

Piling people into shoddy estates with inadequate back-up facilities requiring necessary and constant refurbishment when there is little money available to carry it out is not the long-term answer to housing problems. Yet it is also interesting to note that many of those families who, for example, were subjected for years to the appalling dampness and condensation problems of the notorious Orlet houses in Edinburgh and complained bitterly to little avail, were well satisfied with their community life and did not wish to move or change it. All they wanted was a home free from damp, where the paper did not fall off the walls and where their children did not develop coughs.

The stalag housing of the Sixties, along with grotesque architectural shapes and contortions in the name of progress, which scarred cities and often the people who lived in them, are now assessed as monuments of failure. Yet the kind of thinking that created them still lives. Sons of the Sixties continue to be created as blots throughout Britain today and it is one of the reasons why the public, just like Prince Charles, increasingly question the wisdom of putting their faith in the judgement of architects and planners alone.

In Edinburgh there is a general belief that a great light of understanding dawned too late when the full awfulness of the St James Centre was revealed. The important lesson, it was felt, was so well learned that some architects today scoff at the suggestion that something similar could again be perpetrated on the city. Such confidence! Sadly it is this kind of complacency that demands the need for increased vigilance by those watchdog bodies who scan plans on the city's behalf, for there are no guarantees against a repeat infliction of something so patently not good enough for Edinburgh.

In the central residential communities the pleasure of owning a home in Edinburgh's New Town is blunted by the ever-increasing cost of living in history and preserving it, and by the swamping tide of the motor car, in particular other people's cars. As large companies and speculators survey this central area for office accommodation and the delights of New Town living are increasingly coveted, reflected by soaring property prices, it becomes more difficult for those without financial resources to remain as residents. It is an opportunity not unnoticed by those with an eye for an investment, as the first £100,000 garage indicates; and as house prices have rocketed, so have absentee landlords proliferated while they rent out their accommodation to pay the mortgage and watch their investment grow.

Whether you live in a flat in Westburn or Hailesland Park or a basement in Great King Street or a fourth-floor front in Dundas Street above the growling traffic, or whether you are a Moray Place lawyer or a Broomhouse joiner with different qualities of lives and different aspirations, matters of environment are still inescapable. They may be different in kind, scale, cost and urgency, but they all bear down. As always a balance has to be struck between conservation of the old and the needs of the present. Accomplishing the balance of needs is the difficult and complex task.

Yes, we all know the way to the Forth Road Bridge; getting there is the problem. Like other cities traffic disposal baffles Edinburgh, but with a large residential population at its heart, along with an important financial centre and business community, a daily commuter invasion, a major shopping facility and a roaring tourist trade all crammed into an ancient city the need to find a route out of chaos is urgent.

In the end, of course, plans and buildings and problems of environment are in the main about people. People today are more involved in the quality of their lives than ever before. Quality may be difficult to define, but most people know what they want and when they are satisfied, and they also have different expectations. People today are more determined to achieve them than they have been in the past, and it is those same architects and planners berated by Prince Charles who must help and advise them.

This is a book about Edinburgh's New Town and all the modern-day city-centre pressures associated with the old and the new have been familiar for a very long time. It is easy to oversimplify and it may well be more difficult to renew and refurbish than to build afresh, but perhaps today's problems should be set against two perspectives.

Firstly, they should be set against the enormity of the task in the 18th and 19th centuries when it was decided to break out of the confines of the medieval city and create a whole new town on a greenfield site below the Castle to a classical grand design fit for a capital. It was a noble concept that demanded vision, and a degree of courage and application. It was achieved.

Secondly, once the plans took shape in stone to make one of the finest city centrepieces in Europe, with the additional bonus of the filmset faerie skyline of the Old Town as a backdrop, it was glaringly obvious that not only had Edinburgh inherited a jewel of unique beauty, but also the serious responsibility as well as the accountability of preserving it for posterity. Unfortunately it took many years before the obvious was understood and acted upon. In the interim some fine buildings were lost when they might have been retained.

Of course, modern living is much more complex today — and competitive. Regulations bristle from every quarter, costs have soared, while architects, planners and local authorities have been disciplined into limiting their horizons and thinking small-scale, one eye on screwed-down budgets, the other on the calendar to get the job completed on time so that the next can begin. But it would be wrong to believe that the creators of Edinburgh's New Town 200 years ago did not confront very similar problems. Raising finance has always been difficult, petty minds and petty hold-ups are timeless and universal, and quality of concept, leadership and skill were in as much demand then as they are today. It is in the areas of vision, leadership and the will to surmount problems that we see significant distinctions between then and now on Edinburgh's stage. And enthusiasm. Yet it is interesting to witness the same sense of mission and determination in those who want to preserve the New Town today as in those who wanted to build it all those years ago.

Inevitably, a city cannot stand trapped for ever in a time warp. It must react to change and develop with it. One of the most important features about Edinburgh's New Town is simply that it still lives and it does so vibrantly. It is as much about people as buildings. It has a highly developed community spirit, a strong sense of identity, pride in its historical background, its classical good looks and its achievements. Look behind those splendid facades of banks, financial houses, insurance offices, galleries, shops and all the other fine outer garments of the New Town and the people today continue to bear a strong resemblance to their distant forbears in the Old Town which gave it life.

The famous Edinburgh skyline from Castle down to the crown of St Giles' Cathedral on the left. The view looks over the tree tops in Charlotte Square. The steeple in the centre is the former Tolbooth St John's church, once the highest in Edinburgh. One of these days history will repeat itself and, as happened in Princes Street Gardens, Edinburgh's private gardens will face a campaign to open to the public.

In those days almost the entire socio-economic structure lived up closes in skyscraper 'land' tenements on the Royal Mile: gentry, judges, servants, businessmen, artisans, writers, apothecaries, fleshers, bakers, publicans, advocates, the rich, the poor all passed each other up and down their close stair. Among the 25,000 population of today's New Town almost the same social composition is present, but spread out across two square miles. Perhaps the population today is weighted more heavily towards the professions, certainly it is

13

more cosmopolitan, yet that same essential mix is present right down to a few kenspeckle figures and itinerant homeless, some of whom still sneak into Princes Street Gardens when no-one is looking to shiver the night away on a bench or behind the plastic sheeting on a draughty New Town building site surrounded by Edinburgh's sleeping high society.

In spite of the more enlightened approach to the environment in recent times and the release of more money than ever before to solve problems, environmental pressures are unrelenting. They also change in character and emphasis as more interest is taken by the public. Everyone, it seems, wants to clamber onto the green bandwagon these days. It is reassuring, of course, but it has also become fashionable, and, cynically perhaps, too many professed campaigners appear to be espousing the conservation cause for commercial reasons rather than from conviction. One of the dangers of over-commercialisation in Edinburgh, recognised as one of Britain's leading tourist centres, is that uncontrolled exuberance leads to a cheapening process, the introduction of unnecessary Hollywood razzamatazz, the creation of ersatz history. But Edinburgh has the real thing. It does not need imitation or exaggeration.

Already the ideas are flying to jazz up the Royal Mile. No doubt many improvements can be made to that great thoroughfare of antiquity from Castle down to Palace, but at all costs the authentic must not be compromised. The Royal Mile is unique. It remains a museum of the Scottish centuries that has never been shown off at its best. Its story deserves to be shouted, but not in Disneyesque with a battalion of Bonnie Jeans purveying haggisburgers, crowdie, cock-a-leekie and chips at the old luckenbooths. And what wonders could be achieved with Princes Street and the Gardens! Yeah, it's mega! What a challenge! And the big Christmas switch-on in George Street just proves those old Edinburgh stick-in-the-mud fossils are prepared to change if there's a buck to be made. Yeah, yeah, and we could spread the lights down into those deserted Queen Street Gardens for summer discos.

We trust not. But crazier things have happened and Edinburgh must be on its guard against the further encroachment of the cheap, the plastic, the tawdry and the fake. Promotional ideas become increasingly hyped as commercial pressures grow. Tourism is important to the Edinburgh economy, but Edinburgh's good reputation in the visitor stakes is based on its own authentic qualities: its beauty, its dramatic cityscapes, its excellent facilities and its historic centre. Glitz and glitter are for other cities. Edinburgh neither needs nor wants it, which is not a recommendation to stand still. Edinburgh will and must change. But it must be controlled change and the reins of control must be firmly in the hands of people who know their city and care for it. Edinburgh does need promoting, but not fantasising and certainly not Brigadoon-style kitsch.

A door in Heriot Row . . . No 13 was the first house to be built in the second New Town development and the site was considered so remote that no one would want to live there. But it brought nothing but good luck and nowadays it is one of the most sought-after streets in Edinburgh. Many of the original features remain intact. It faces the private Queen Street Gardens at the front and Robert Louis Stevenson could have watched the ships in the Forth from the upper rear windows of No 17. It remains the epitome of elegant living.

The challenges ahead are all about building on our rich inheritance. We are fortunate to have it. Others envy it. Both in the city centre and the rest of Edinburgh an enormous development programme is taking place. It creates the opportunity to take a fresh look and ask again what kind of city we want for the future. The critical question is this: will it be good enough for Scotland's capital?

In parts of the city the changes are already far advanced with some buildings of quality in the modern idiom that are encouraging and welcome and a credit to Edinburgh as well as to those who conceived and built them. But some opportunities have been missed and it must be hoped others will also rise to the challenge and do better.

In the city centre Edinburgh's history, heritage and tradition must be the guideline. When there is doubt about the direction of progress, the answer is to look back and use Edinburgh's past to confirm the way ahead.

In the ongoing debate on future development and the handling of change in Edinburgh the voices on all sides should be heard. And if the Prince of Wales wants to contribute, then good for him. At least he cares and is prepared to speak out while others remain silent. In Scotland the right of the individual to hold a viewpoint and try to convince others of its merit is still important. More voices should be heard. Edinburgh is awash with people of calibre who have a contribution to make. They should make it. There should be more opinion, more frank talking. More sparks should fly.

A few years ago, the then Lord Provost of Glasgow, fresh from a successful campaign to convince the world that his city was miles better than it used to be, issued Edinburgh with a challenge. Clean up the Scott Monument, he said, and let it be a symbol of a new intent to have the whole of Edinburgh pulling together as a team to its greater benefit. Pulling together has not been one of the strengths of Scotland's capital, but there are signs at last that things may be stirring in that direction. Now with the grime of more than a century removed the Scott Monument will indeed shine out as a symbol. It is up to the people of Edinburgh, however, and particularly those who hold the reins of power, to decide what eventually that symbol will represent by the course that the city takes.

OPPOSITE

Looking out on Charlotte Square . . . the country extremity of the first New Town and one of its finest features. Craig did the planning, Adam the design with modification by Robert Reid and it took some 13 years to complete. Adam's fee was £200 with five guineas for each house plan. The square was not completed until 28 years after his death. Adam's design for St George's Church was recast by Reid, perhaps to its detriment, but today it is West Register House and it is a pity some other notable empty Edinburgh churches could not be put to such good use. Charlotte Square has been hailed as 'one of the major achievements in European civic architecture' of the time, but what Lord Cockburn remembered was its attractive rural setting and the sound of the corncrakes in the green fields beyond.

CHAPTER ONE

IN THE
BEGINNING

'DUN-EDIN! oh, how altered now!
Where safe amid thy mountain court
Thou sitt'st, like Empress at her sport,
And liberal, unconfined, and free,
Flinging thy white arms to the sea.'

Sir Walter Scott.

THE grandstand view of Scotland's capital is not from the Castle ramparts or even the summit of Arthur's Seat, that long-extinct volcano like a lion crouching above the city. The Edinburgh perspective is seen at its most spectacular from the craggy knoll of the Calton Hill, the platform for the classical columns of the ruined Greek temple which catches the eye and curiosity of Princes Street paraders. It is all that was built of the national war memorial to the fallen in the Napoleonic Wars before the money ran out. But although it has been the raw material of a century of after-dinner and music-hall snickers at the city's expense, those twelve elegant pillars of best Craigleith sandstone nonetheless grace Edinburgh with an almost theatrical backdrop along with the upturned telescope of the Nelson Monument and the Doric columns of the New Observatory up there beside it. In fact, the National Monument probably does more for Edinburgh in its state of instant ruin than if it had been completed.

The view from the top of the Calton Hill is dramatic. This was Robert Louis Stevenson's favourite prospect of his city, where the east wind is at its draughtiest and Edinburgh is wrapped around you so that with the merest turn of the head new panoramas declare themselves in exclamation and range in every direction. Here are the stage-sets of Scott's 'own romantic town', the old and new jostling in close proximity for recognition, all around a massive pointing of spires, domes, towers and turrets, a permanent retrospective of Edinburgh's history and memories and aspirations through the centuries.

This is the spot where the visitors' cameras click on the top of Calton Hill overlooking Princes Street in the centre of the picture. The monument to Dugald Stewart is on the right. Below left is the rocky promontory known in olden times as the Miller's Knowe or the Dow Craig, possibly from the Gaelic Dhu — the Black Craig. A public hanging took place here in 1554 and the City Accounts have the itemised bill: '. . . for taking of ane gret gibet furth of the Nether Tolbooth, to haif hangit hommill (beardless) Jok on, and bringing it again to Sanct Paullis Wark. Item for cords to bynd and hang him with . . .'.

It was over there, for example, on the Royal Mile, a few hundred yards away, where John Knox lived and sent chill into the hearts of his St Giles' congregation, where later Jenny Geddes hurled her well-aimed stool; round the corner the National Covenant was signed among the gravestones of Greyfriars Church, where a small Skye terrier called Bobby touched the hearts of city councillors; over the wall and into the gardens of George Heriot's School, where Cromwell placed his cannon to lay siege to Edinburgh Castle and balloonist Vincenzo

Lunardi began his flight across the Forth; along the Royal Mile where Prince Charles Edward Stewart rode in short-lived triumph with his Highland horde and the dignified Montrose was dragged on a sled in humiliation to his execution just out of sight at the Mercat Cross; down the closes where Robert Burns caroused in Dawney Douglas's tavern with the Crochallan Fencibles and in the Canongate where Clarinda lies buried; along the corridors of the Palace of Holyrood, where Rizzio's cries were cut short as the dirks struck, and when the Royal pennant flies today you know the Royal family are in their Edinburgh home; the screams of the 'witches' burned at the stake echoed up from Greenside, directly below the Calton Hill, where jousts once took place, to mingle with those of the 300 who died by fire on Castlehill; into the New Town, where Dr James Y. Simpson experimented with a sinister phial of liquid called chloroform at his home in Queen Street; on George Street, among the fine banks and financial houses, where Sir Walter Scott in a precious Edinburgh literary happening announced to an astonished gathering that he was the secret author of the Waverley Novels; and across the road where the Disruption that split the Kirk began in St Andrew's Church.

Some cityscape, some stage, some cast!

Just below is Princes Street, still one of Europe's most attractive thoroughfares, but now a river of stop-go-crawl cars and maroon buses; the Scott Monument in the Gardens sticks up like a giant rocket waiting for ignition, while the ancient Castle confronts a foreign army of tourist invaders, clambering over the battlements, faces peering from defensive positions reminiscent of earlier days. George Street and Queen Street, the hub of the 200-year-old New Town, are clogged with slow-motion vehicles, the throng rushing like ants to shops, trains, buses, offices, boardrooms as a big commercial capital goes about its daily darg, with the small consolation that unlike other cities Edinburgh's traffic jams are at least aesthetically pleasing, disciplined into the geometric parallelograms, intersections, squares, circles and crescents of New Town planning magnificence.

OPPOSITE

The heights of Edinburgh . . . the old and the new of the New Town meet on Princes Street. In spite of the rushing clock on the tower of the old North British Hotel, now the refurbished Balmoral, the timelessness and grandeur of past centuries remain aloft. The columns of the National Gallery on Calton Hill, the upturned telescope of the Nelson Monument beside it, the clock tower and the Scott Monument continue the vertical theme that gives a new meaning to Stevenson's 'precipitous city'. Two centuries ago Georgie Boyd's 'mud brig' was right of the Royal Scottish Academy; a century ago the traffic was horse-and-carriage and horse-drawn trams; today it is over-loaded streets and combative driving throughout central Edinburgh.

Close-up of the National Monument showing its twelve classical columns of Craigleith sandstone. Its foundation stone was laid to coincide with the famous visit of George IV to Edinburgh. With cannons roaring in salute from the Castle one of the dedication inscription plates summed up the fervour of the day: 'To the glory of God, in honour of the King, for the good of the people, this monument, this tribute of a grateful country to her gallant and illustrious sons, as a memorial of the past and incentive to the future heroism of the men of Scotland, was founded on the 27th day of August in the year of our Lord 1822 . . .'. It cost around £1000 per column before the money ran out (*Royal Commission on Ancient and Historical Monuments, Scotland*).

OPPOSITE

A skyview of all the Calton Hill features in one picture: in the centre is the old Royal Observatory, the original three-storey tower is in the corner nearest the camera by James Craig, and the second, in the centre of the square in the shape of a St George's Cross, is by the prolific William Playfair. Just in front the little monument to Professor Dugald Stewart is also by Playfair. The National Monument, again by Playfair, is to the rear with the Nelson Monument on its right. Just visible in the top right hand corner is the old Royal High School by Thomas Hamilton. The broad sweep of Regent Road passes the old Calton Burying Ground where many famous names in the Edinburgh story are at rest, and St Andrew's House is on the right.

Sir James Young Simpson — from his home at 52 Queen Street he became a celebrated medical figure of world renown. Now associated with chloroform experiments his pioneering work in gynaecology is less well remembered, yet he was Professor of Midwifery at Edinburgh University at the age of 28.

Standing on the Calton Hill around 1878, when his *Picturesque Notes* were first published, Stevenson's attention was drawn to the incongruity of sheep browsing around him in the centre of the city; the boys from the Royal High School were playing in the yards below while a few steps away the female prisoners were taking exercise 'like a string of nuns' in the new jail; a red-coated sentry smartly paced to and fro on guard at the entrance to Holyrood Palace; tall sailing ships still tacked up the Forth to join the forest of masts at Leith; trains trailing clouds of steam clanked in the valley; chimney sweeps did their delicate balancing act on nearby rooftops; washday sheets and blankets fluttered and cracked in the breeze all around; there was a multitude of sounds like the steady thwack-thwack of carpets being beaten, the jingle of tramway bells, the ringing out of many clocks across the city and, as evening closed in, the gas 'lichties' made their rounds and lit up the lamps with a little plop, a sight that had lived with him since childhood as night fell on his home in the New Town.

When viewed from the Old Town, where some 200 years ago those first far-sighted Edinburgh planners contemplated the green fields, browsing cattle, small farms and thatched cottages that lay below their overcrowded spine of rock and envisaged the future expansion of Edinburgh, the striking situation of the Calton Hill was obvious. Correctly it was singled out for special attention. They were men of vision in those days and determined to create the new Edinburgh in a style and quality fit for Scotland's capital. The Calton Hill was therefore envisaged almost as a symbolic site to reflect all that was glorious during Edinburgh's remarkable classical development in the second half of the 18th century. Although woods and copses studded the northern outlook, Calton Hill itself always appeared denuded of trees. Sometimes it was called the Black Craig after its volcanic rocky face, and Miller's Knowe was its southern promontory. The Quarry Holes, where at one time stone was excavated, was the secluded place for duels and fist-fight settlement of private arguments. Public hangings took place on the hill, the Carmelite monastery of Greenside was on its west side, although no trace now remains, and the rat-tatting of the Fairy Boy's drum could be heard to summon particular elves for their weekly gathering on the bald summit or, at least, that was the superstition.

From early days two well-used roads had stretched down to the Port of Leith from below the Old Town, but in the middle of the 18th century, when the first steps were taken to expand Edinburgh northwards, a long, straight country road between two low drystone walls called the Lang Dykes or the Lang Gait stood where the throng on Princes Street scurries about its business today. To be precise, it may have been nearer the line of Rose Street, but the difference in position was only a matter of yards. A collection of cottages, a farm and manor house called Moultray's Hill was where Register House is now situated. On maps and documents of the day Moultray's Hill takes a number of different spellings, but no one seemed much to mind and local folk certainly knew where it was. The site where the Royal Bank of Scotland's head office stands was occupied by a cottage called 'Peace and Plenty', near Gabriel's Road, where those out for an afternoon stroll in summer could refresh themselves with strawberries and cream or curds. The present St George's Church was built in the middle of what was Bearford's Park, and Wemyss Place replaced Wood's Farm, which stretched down to Cannon Mills and offered an excellent day's shooting for snipe, woodcock and partridges. The fields which today are Queen Street and Heriot Row provided

25

Sir Walter Scott — he is remembered as a writer but his enthusiasms and love of Scotland had a profound influence on the development of Edinburgh. The original high ideals of the New Town were preserved and enhanced by his free-flow of ideas and desire for improvement. His house in North Castle Street is now a legal office.

particularly good wheat crops and it is recorded that hares started up from the feet of all who went for a country walk around Wood's Farm.

Much of the area between the Old Town and the Forth was rough country moorland, marsh and ridges of tussocky grass, with patches of gorse, whin and woodland, outcropping rock and deep ravines. It was criss-crossed with lonely country tracks quickly vacated as darkness fell. St Cuthbert's Church, under the Castle's north-west cliff, had been there before records were kept and was probably founded in the eighth century. The Kirk Loan stretched from it — the same site as today's St Cuthbert's Church — down to the wooden Stokebridge, as it was then called, and on to the ford across the Water of Leith behind the present Malta Terrace. Kirkbrae led from St Cuthbert's Church down to Drumsheugh, where the imposing Drumsheugh House stood, which gave shelter to the Chevalier Johnstone, ADC to Bonnie Prince Charlie, after Culloden, until he could be spirited away to safety. The village of Broughton was seen as being so far distant that some people went there for their summer holidays and Broughton Loan was the road they took. It was along the line of the Lang Dykes that Claverhouse and his troopers rode in 1689, where Bonnie Prince Charlie's scouts reconnoitred the city in 1745, and it is recounted that a highwayman once did business at pistol point where the buses run today.

Immediately below the Castle was the Nor' Loch, at one time the haunt of giant eels that for ten merks a year became part of the diet of the Trinity Hospital. It was a great attraction to waterfowl, a favourite boating pond in summer and skating rink in winter until three men died when the ice cracked. By the middle decades of the 18th century, however, it had degenerated into a huge open and repugnant sewer. Those intending suicide once sought its dark waters, but as it became a receptacle for gardyloo, the gory leftovers from nearby slaughter-houses, stray dogs, deceased cats and garbage in general, they looked elsewhere rather than face its multifarious odours. Because the Nor' Loch was deep, fetid and a place for Edinburgh's undesirables to foregather, it was an obvious obstacle to the development of the old city northwards.

For long Edinburgh on its rocky ridge had thought only defensively. Considerations of expansion had been inhibited by the religious strife and civil war that had bedevilled Scotland for centuries. But at last the warring came to an end and with the 'Forty-Five uprising reaching such an inglorious conclusion on Culloden Moor, suddenly Scotland found herself uneasily yet indisputably in a state of reassuring and unaccustomed peace. With so much energy having been concentrated so negatively on conflict, the realisation that the future apparently looked secure was at first slow to dawn. Then things began to happen at the rush. With the peace came the beginning of increased prosperity; with peace came the opportunity for Scotland to reappraise itself as a nation — 'This is an historical age and we are the historical people', said philosopher David Hume; and with peace came such energy, such confidence, such curiosity, such creativity, such a flowering of Scottish genius in so many directions it was as if Scotland was trying to make up for lost time.

How the West End looked before the New Town was built . . . the ancient church of St Cuthbert's stands outside the city's defences on the edge of the Nor' Loch, cattle graze, ducks and moorhen nest in the reeds and the Castle Rock reflects in the still waters. Today it is the scene of West Princes Street Gardens and the railway line. The Nor' Loch's waters were indeed still for it was the repository of local slaughter houses and the deposits of the over-crowded city above.

There was no longer need for a walled town. The population soared, which made the confines and conditions of the old Edinburgh almost intolerable. It became one of the most overcrowded cities in Europe, building upwards, smaller and more cramped, but never sideways. Dank, dirty 'laigh rooms' or underground

Before the streets came . . . looking over Picardy Village and Gayfield House to the Forth and the Fife hills beyond. Then it was grazing ground and sailing ships plying out of Leith. Now it is Picardy Place, York Place, Forth and Albany Streets with Gayfield Square the site of a sub-division of Lothian and Borders Police. Picardy Place was named after a colony of French silk weavers who attempted to establish a trade here in the 17th century.

basements were all too often used as nurseries, and what with the lack of sanitation in the city it was little wonder that the infant mortality rate was a scandal. One night in September 1751, the side-wall entrance of a six-storey 'land' tenement collapsed and the resultant survey of property disclosed that some of it was in such a dangerous state that demolition was the only answer. Although plans were discussed for a phased knock-down and replacement policy, the pressures to build anew elsewhere could no longer be resisted.

The first positive step to break out of Edinburgh's ancient high-ground stronghold and expand was taken in 1752 when 'The Proposals for carrying on certain Public Works in the city of Edinburgh' were published. Although the unsightly piles of rubble where tenements were being razed for public safety were obvious daily reminders of the need for speed, 'The Proposals' carefully set down in detail the logical reasons and arguments why development of a new Edinburgh should begin quickly both north and southwards.

It was at once obvious that 'The Proposals' were well prepared, which gave them immediate authority. Those involved had done their research thoroughly. They had surveyed what was happening elsewhere in Britain and Europe and what was not happening in Edinburgh. Berlin and Turin were reported to be thinking big and carrying out public works of a high order, but in particular that other capital city to the far south was making such enormous improvements and of such quality that it made Edinburgh, Scotland's capital, at best look laggard, lacking in initiative, and uncouth in comparison. Doubt was even cast on Edinburgh's capability of improving itself. So cleverly national pride was engaged at the outset and the challenge set and the city chided for its meanness, its lack of horizon and decision-making; a vision was unveiled of the great fillip and stimulation development would mean to the arts, to business, trade and to the rest of Scotland; the presentation was couched in grandiose terms of splendid buildings, but also care was taken to explain what the 'improvements' would mean to ordinary people.

In their way 'The Proposals' were a work of genius. It was not that they dealt in detail with how the new town should look, but it was their clear-minded and uncompromising setting of standards and aspirations that was important. They were a declaration of faith and were delivered with conviction. In part they were fanciful, part cold logic, in part they overflowed with idealism and national pride, which has always been a volatile mixture Scotland has found difficult to resist. Some eyes glinted as commercial instincts were engaged, for middle-class ambition could not be disguised. The basic and honest motivation behind 'The Proposals' was obvious, however, and it was all about creating a new Edinburgh of distinction in the best interests of the capital city, its citizens and Scotland. It was also a clarion call for nationwide support both financially and in spirit.

Now think of today. Think of the number of plans, miniature in comparison, that over the years have been produced to improve Edinburgh — plans about roads, buildings, recreation areas, car parks, use of disused railway lines, new housing schemes, industrial sites, even opera houses — all sentenced to dust-gather in some planning department filing cabinet. Perhaps that or the bucket was the best place for some, but others were worthy and came to nothing for the wrong reasons. Think of the excuses that have been deployed over the years and the energy expended to have so many delayed indefinitely or scrapped. Think of the work that went into their creation, the aggravation of having them frustrated. Edinburgh retains a talent for procrastination that can be stifling, and it was evident even when 'The Proposals' were published.

But walk around the New Town now, examine again closely the grand design, the fine array of buildings, some of them masterpieces, the beauty and dignity, those sudden little excitements of an unexpected glimpse of the Castle or the Calton Hill or Arthur's Seat or the green trees and flowers of Princes Street Gardens or out across the rooftops over the Forth to Fife. Compare it with other cities. Then think of those wheat-fields and the swamps, the jagged cliffs, the gorse-covered slopes like today's Arthur's Seat or the Pentlands, because that is how it was before the streets and people came. Then consider how difficult it seems today to build something worthwhile, something that lasts, and wonder at the task of accomplishing the New Town.

So often dreams and schemes are mere flights of imagination and never quite materialise. Sometimes, of course, they lack only the special individual who can make them happen, and without him or her there is failure. As with all great enterprises, the building of the New Town therefore urgently required a leader, someone exceptional to take decisions, encourage or force others to follow. The natural leader to take command was the Lord Provost. As Edinburgh's first citizen the Lord Provost's contacts and influence throughout the city were of major importance, but personal qualities as much as office were critical for a project of such scale. Chance also has its card to play, and by chance Lord Provost George Drummond was found to be the man with the full hand of qualities demanded for the task. Thrawn, likeable, able, respected, Perthshire-born Drummond's passion and ambition were single-mindedly for his adopted city. A Whig and kirk elder, he had fought at Sheriffmuir, and fled with the rest of General Johnny Cope's sprinters at Prestonpans, which probably showed his good sense at the time. Drummond was also the arch-politician. A government man all his days, he had been instrumental in giving Edinburgh an infirmary back in 1725, and because of his talents and service he was six times Lord Provost. In over 200 years Edinburgh has never had another quite like him.

'The Proposals' set out four main objectives: to build an Exchange on the north side of the High Street; to erect on the ruins of Parliament Close a building for courts, the town council, several registers and the Advocates' Library. The dramatic part came next: 'to obtain an act of parliament for extending the royalty to enlarge and beautify the town by opening new streets to the north and south, removing the markets and shambles, and turning the North-loch into a canal, with walks and terraces on each side'. It was a matter-of-fact statement. By today's standards it was sensational. It led directly to the building of Edinburgh's New Town.

Lastly — and naturally — it was suggested that the costs should be defrayed by a national contribution. A year after 'The Proposals' were published Lord Provost Drummond was into his stride. The first of the new buildings, the Exchange, now the centre of the City Chambers in the Old Town, was underway.

There had been talk of development plans for years, of course, because city overspill was correctly interpreted as inevitable. One of the early visions was

George Drummond — he was elected Lord Provost six times and became one of the most influential figures in Edinburgh's history. It was Drummond who forced the pace to create the New Town and set the standards to ensure it was built with distinction.

produced by the Earl of Mar, who had been exiled for his part in the 1715 Jacobite uprising. What he envisaged in the 1720s had many similarities to the final outcome, and included both a north and south bridge, although his imaginative plan to turn the Nor' Loch into a canal was never fulfilled. As the Old Town's population increased, the pressure for a bridge became urgent. Without proper access to the proposed new residential development across the loch the plan would certainly fail. Trade into Leith was also increasing, and easing the arduous horse-and-cart journey up the hill from the Port to the Old Town was seen as a high priority. The urgency demanded action. In 1759 drainage of the Nor' Loch began, and three years later George Drummond laid the foundation stone of the North Bridge.

Haggling about costs has to be part of the rich Edinburgh experience, it seems, and it was no different in the mid-18th century. The same exaggerated brow-clutching, the same tired arguments that have so often resulted in a standstill were shouted as shrilly then as nowadays or as far back as living memory carries in Edinburgh. It would have been pleasing to record that the building of the New Town went without a hitch, that all sides threw themselves into the task and miraculously the proud new Edinburgh sprouted from the ground. It was not like that. As ever the uncertainty of finance was an ongoing problem. Bickering, hesitancy, politics, personal animosities, difficult individuals, pettiness — the full range of frustrations that still characterises the process of local authority decision-making — came into play. It is to the undying credit of those who made the decisions in those days that they would not be deterred.

What was needed now was a detailed plan. Not just any plan, but something that would capture the hopes envisaged in 'The Proposals'. Without the right plan all those brave words would mean nothing. Its importance therefore assumed almost intimidating proportions. With fingers crossed, the call went out in the spring of 1766 inviting submissions. Six people accepted the challenge. The reward for their efforts was deemed to be more in honour than in riches, for the accolade of having been judged best was a gold medal impressed with the arms of the city of Edinburgh and 'the freedom of the city in a silver box'. The plan by Mr James Craig, a little-known architect, was judged by the Lord Provost, assisted by Mr John Adam, as the most appropriate.

It was, of course, a momentous decision. Although it was hardly universally acclaimed at the time, it nonetheless provided Edinburgh with the classical blueprint that the city sought. It projected Craig into public prominence, and although it remains a pity that the five other designs have never been found for comparison Craig's plan has withstood the test of time.

Yet history has not been kind to Craig. Doubts over his true ability continue to this day. Is Edinburgh's fair face and splendid use of space the result of good

James Craig — his plan for the New Town became the talking point of Europe and put his stamp on Edinburgh for ever. His achievement was only grudgingly admitted and the precocious 23-year-old quickly fell from public esteem and died in poverty.

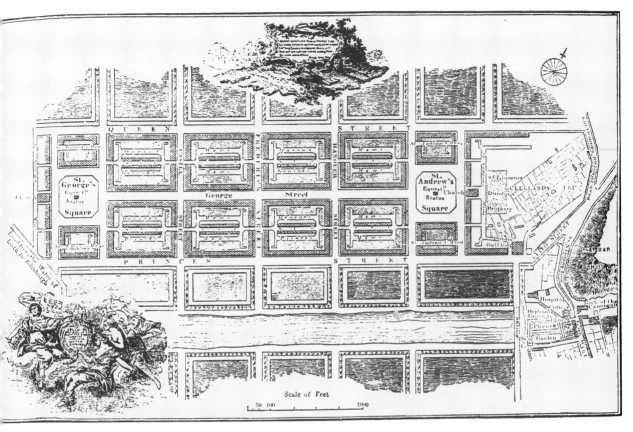

James Craig's prizewinning plan for the New Town was superimposed onto the grassy ridge with its outcropping rock that is now George Street. At the time the plan was criticised as no more than a series of draughty parallelograms, but its sensitive use of space in relation to the Castle, the Old Town skyline, Calton Hill and the Fife panorama across the Forth at once gave the expanded Edinburgh the drama and grandeur of a stage setting.

luck, the assiduous copying of the work of others, go the arguments, or was he truly touched by real ability? Was his plan a moment of inspiration that, sadly, was never repeated? Sometimes architects find it difficult to be kind to each other, and it may be that Craig's reputation has suffered unfairly. Perhaps he brought much of the doubt and criticism on his own shoulders. His manner, it seems, was precocious, arrogant and demanding, which ensured uneasy relationships. Craig was still in his 20s when his plan was selected, and whether or not inexperience or youthful exuberance played a part, his dealings with the Town Council were frequently brittle. In the end it proved a tactical misjudgement. It may be that Craig's uncle, James Thomson, who had distinguished himself as a poet and was author of the jingoistic 'Rule Britannia', influenced him into a mistaken sense of family superiority. At any rate, contention and argument seemed to follow at his heels and as time passed his star waned, he fell on hard times and eventually died unremarked and in debt. The Old Observatory on Calton Hill is a remaining example of his work, although even he would be unlikely to acclaim its merits.

Nonetheless, by talent or luck Craig's plan disciplined the growth of the New Town into a mould that at once gave it grandeur, grace, space and harmony. The concept of two large elegant squares — St Andrew Square and Charlotte Square — joined by the straight, wide and handsome thoroughfare of George Street, with less important streets running parallel and intersecting it, may not have been original, but when superimposed on Edinburgh's hilly contours Craig's imaginative use of space is immediately obvious and he should be given credit for it.

In addition, his two one-sided streets — Princes Street and Queen Street — designed to take best advantage of the dramatic hanging valley below the Castle and the serrated Old Town skyline to the south and the Fife vistas to the north again demonstrate an astute awareness of void as applied to the local terrain. It is claimed that the concept of streets with houses on one side (only half a street, claimed some detractors) was hardly new, and the pleasant city of Bath is indicated as an example of where it has worked well. But where is the effect put to better use than in the city of Edinburgh?

Although Craig is unlikely to have designed individual houses for his plan, another reason for the New Town's handsome looks is the use of the light-coloured calciferous sandstone found in quantity in the quarries of Barnton, Craigleith, Hailes and Ravelston. Most of the paving stones came from Hailes, but the Craigleith stone was held in such high regard that it was sent south in giant loads for the building of Buckingham Palace and the British Museum in London.

Originally, when the streets were being named, without reference Craig took it upon himself to give the name St Giles Street to what we now know as Princes Street. The Town Council was furious. Even George III protested because he feared it would be associated with a particularly squalid London street of the same name. St Giles Street quickly changed to Princes Street, named after the future George IV and the Duke of York. George Street, named after the king, was envisaged as the main street in Craig's plan, and the two lesser parallel streets flanking it were called Thistle Street and Rose Street after the emblems of England and Scotland. Later Frederick Street was also given a royal connection after the Prince of Wales.

In January of 1765 architects 'and others' were invited to submit plans for a bridge, and the successful designer would receive 30 guineas or a gold medal

The old and the new . . . the bridge that leads from the hideous St James Centre across busy Leith Street towards the Calton Hill. The St James Centre and the bridge would have Craig, Adam, Playfair and the rest of the New Town architects in tears today at the way in which standards and aspirations have been discarded. At the top of the hill is what Robert Louis Stevenson called a 'field of monuments', symbols to an age which brought people from all over Europe to see Edinburgh's New Town.

to that value for his efforts. There were seven entries and the Bridge Committee chose the plan produced by Edinburgh architect David Henderson. Not for the first time, however, where matters of prestige or large sums of money are involved, second thoughts seemed to prevail. To his surprise Henderson found that estimates were being sought not only for his design but also for the plans of

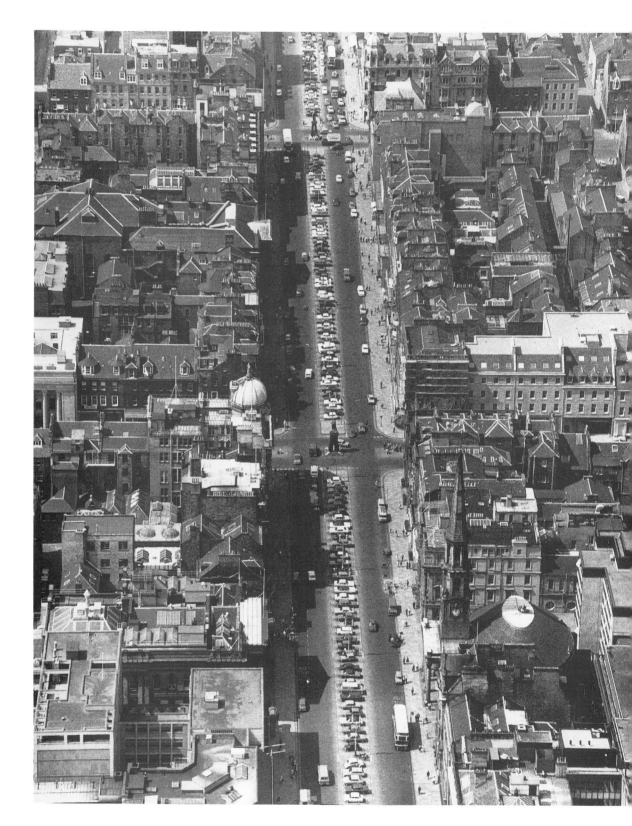

one of the committee members, William Mylne. What happened behind the scenes may never be known, but six months later it was announced that Mylne's plans, with some alterations by John Adam, had been accepted. They were, of course, the cheapest estimates. Four weeks later the contract was signed.

Apart from 'The Proposals', the erection of the North Bridge was the single most significant factor in the expansion northwards of Edinburgh. Its importance for the future as well as for the build-up of pressure in the Old Town, where conditions were becoming increasingly squalid as too many people tried to crowd into too few houses, is demonstrated by the emphasis on early completion. 'Speed the bridge' became almost a city slogan for all parties involved, and a target date of November 1769 was set for the opening. The contract price for the 1,134-feet-long, 70-feet high bridge was £10,140. Steady progress was made, the first arch was completed in June 1768, and early in the following year delighted pedestrians were allowed to cross over to 'the other side' for a stroll along the Lang Dykes. Suddenly interest soared and prospective residents began seriously to consider a 'flitting' from Old Town to New.

In August 1769 tragedy struck. Part of the south abutment collapsed and five bodies were discovered under the rubble. Not only was it bad news for the image of the new bridge as well as the reputation of the builder, but the project was also thrown into a messy tangle of delay and financial wrangling over additional costs, which continued long after it was open. The total cost of building the North Bridge, including additional sums following the accident, was around £16,000, not even the price of a flat in town today. Such have been the pressures of inflation on cost structures over almost 220 years that the cost of the recent refurbishment and repairs to today's North Bridge, with its floodlit colourful new image, was around £2,000,000. Among sighs of relief, North Bridge was declared at last complete in 1772. With the grand design in place, the door to the development of Edinburgh's New Town was thrown wide open and it was time to start building.

From the outset sights were aimed high. The quality of Craig's plan impressed so much that a prestigious first public development was sought that would set the standard and tone for the New Town to follow. At that time the public records of Scotland were kept in two damp, rat-nibbled laigh rooms below the courts. It was

OPPOSITE

It's high noon on George Street by the clock on St Andrew's and St George's church and inevitably the central parking places are full. A few cars hazard the wardens' attentions and even from 200 feet the pigeons can see the yellow lines clearly. George Street and not Princes Street was planned as the main thoroughfare of the New Town, but at that time it was being developed as quality housing to ease the overcrowding in the Old Town. The building programme progressed westwards.

The wild country viewed from the Old Town that had once been the Lang Dyke is now becoming the sophisticated New Town. Carriages await customers, but many of the residents had their own carriage transport and today's elegant mews flats were the stables. An iron railing runs the length of Princes Street, and houses — not shops — were the buildings facing the Old Town. It did not take long before aspiring New Towners were gazing back on their more humble beginnings disbelievingly and some would rather not remember.

agreed that these important but disintegrating documents should be properly housed in a building of distinction. A site was agreed facing the end of the new North Bridge and with the help of £12,000 from the Treasury, mostly money from the forfeited estates of the Jacobites after the 'Forty-Five, the decision was taken to build Register House.

For a project of such importance careful consideration had to be given to the choice of architect. In offering the Register House brief to Kirkcaldy-born Robert Adam, one of the leading architects of his day in Britain, it was signalled loud and clear that there would be no compromise in creating the New Town as a symbol of quality. There was no need for Adam to return to Scotland because his reputation and fame were already well-established in London and risk was attached to something so idealistic as Edinburgh's New Town with its obvious economic hazards. Yet the ambitious and sophisticated Adam became caught up in the spirit of adventure abroad in his capital city and he immediately saw the possibilities in Craig's masterplan. As it turned out, Adam's talent and accomplishments in Edinburgh spread his fame onto the European stage and he became the most distinguished architect of his generation. Thousands now pass Register House every day and it is largely taken for granted with hardly a sideways glance, yet at the time it was probably one of the finest buildings in Britain since Wren's day. In spite of a chronic cash shortage — it was labelled the most magnificent pigeon house in Europe at one stage when work stopped for six years — Register House has a majestic beauty entirely of its own and is justifiably recognised as one of Adam's most outstanding works.

The successful development of the New Town depended, of course, on private individuals having the confidence to take up feus and build their own houses. But when the Edinburgh magistrates first called for would-be new residents to step forward, the cautious Old Towners were slow to respond. Craig's plan was put on public display for a month at the Council Chambers, and although a few citizens did purchase feus, the hoped-for rush was not forthcoming. Images of remoteness surrounded those draughty braes across the bridge and in the minds of over-crowded but confirmed city dwellers thoughts of outpost Moultray's Hill in the Wild Country and the Lang Dykes road to nowhere began to give them pause. For a time they saw themselves far removed from friends, neighbours and businesses. And what would they do when it rained and they were caught twixt old and new towns, they wondered, or when winter's winds began to snap? The early pioneering enthusiasms appeared to be waning.

At last the magistrates offered an inducement of £20 to the person who would build the first house in the New Town, and for the record it was a Mr John Young who was first in the field, so to speak, with a mansion in Rose Court, George Street. Such was the celebration that James Craig himself came over to lay the foundation stone and the important date was October 26, 1767. The first completed building in the New Town, however, was Thistle Court, still in use behind a wrought-iron railing with a thistle motif and a big No 1 on its nameplate. In burnished brass it also declares today that the offices of Thomson and Baxters W.S. are within, and the top floor is shared with the Consul General of Greece and a number of businesses.

The first house on Princes Street was erected by a Mr John Neale, a local silk dealer, who gave it to his son-in-law, and later it became the Crown Hotel. It is recorded that a Mr Shadrach Moyes built his house on Princes Street but then discovered that the ridge winds indeed had teeth, so he ordered another a little farther along to give him shelter. One of the first of a long line of lawyers to take up residence in the New Town had his home in St Andrew Square, but to his annoyance Mr Wight found his view of the St Giles' clock was about to be lost as Princes Street developed. It was imperative, he explained, to regulate his movements in the morning by observing the clock so that he would not be late for his attendance at Parliament House — he therefore built a second house on Princes Street in direct line so that he could control its height and arrive at work on time. As confidence increased, the idea of 'emigrating over the bridge' became increasingly attractive and the building of the New Town began at last to make steady progress.

The New Town grew out of the east because the bridge provided easy access to the commerce and shopping of the Old Town and reached out westwards towards the rough ground that was to become Charlotte Square. The development of St Andrew Square in particular created interest and made good speed. There was a controversy at the time when it was discovered the east side had been feued by the wealthy Sir Laurence Dundas, who had managed to keep his purchase secret. One of the main features of Craig's plan was two handsome churches facing each other on St Andrew Square and Charlotte Square across the length of the ramrod George Street. Sir Laurence's piece of entrepreneurial manipulation turned out happily, however, for the Dundas three-storey mansion to the design of Sir William Chambers was one of the finest of the New Town and today it is the magnificent and historic headquarters of the Royal Bank of Scotland.

In those early days, of course, Princes Street was entirely residential like the rest of the New Town. It embraced Craig's concept of planning unity, and because of its splendid outlook houses were soon in demand. They conformed to the pattern of three storeys with a sunken area in front, and had iron railings. Perhaps because at that time Princes Street was seen as being of less importance than George Street, the Town Council allowed their planning regulations to be consistently flouted, resulting in an unevenness of quality. By 1781 the more fastidious St Andrew Square was complete, and by 1790 Princes Street, George Street and Queen Street had advanced as far as Hanover Street and were approaching what would be Castle Street. At this point the Town Council had had enough of watching the wilful disregard of their planning guidelines and asserted their authority by issuing strict controls coupled with financial penalties if they were transgressed. All buildings in the principal streets were to be three storeys high, exclusive of garrets and basements, and the whole no higher than 48 feet. Mews' lanes were to be kept for stables or coaches and the houses on Rose and Thistle Streets were not to exceed two storeys.

Horses, coaches! Already in the space of little more than a dozen years the trappings of sophistication were coming to that windy ridge. A way of life was

The elegant St Andrew Square was completed in 1781 and was a magnet to top people. In those days Edinburgh was regarded as a genuine European capital and because communications were so poor it was natural for the nobility and wealthy to seek a town house in Edinburgh rather than London. At one time residents feared the 136-foot column in the centre to Henry Dundas, Viscount Melville — the 'Uncrowned King of Scotland' as wags of the day sarcastically named him — might topple over, but after careful examination engineer Robert Stevenson declared it safe.

changing as New Towners found the old social whirl and habits of the teeming Old Town impossible to continue in their spacious new surroundings. They were forced to seek new entertainments, find new friends, develop a new social order and pattern. The elegant tea and coffee ritual of middle-class close life gave way to the genteel dinner party, even musical and literary evenings, with suitable recitations and songs, although many of the menfolk were still glad to see the backs of the ladies so they could get on with the serious drinking, which was still a way of life. As with cars today, coaches had their own positions of status, and some very fine coaches and well-groomed horses and groomsmen began to appear around St Andrew Square and George Street, which became something of a fashion parade: pavement-sweeping costumes, parasols and elegant hats for the ladies; toppers, fancy waistcoats and canes for the men. Even maidservants, who before the move to the New Town had been content to wear plain clothes, began to appear in 'silk, caps, ribbons, ruffles, false-hair and flounced petticoates'. Beside the railings at the south side of Princes Street a 'taxi rank' of hansom cabs, a few even with high strutters between the shafts, waited for customers.

As families settled in, it was also important that they had somewhere to worship without having to trek back to the Royal Mile every Sunday and possibly even during the week. Because Sir Laurence Dundas had successfully hijacked the St Andrew Square site, this left an important decision to be made on where the church should now be situated. It had, it was felt, at the very least to be in a prominent position on the showpiece George Street and eventually it was located opposite Craig's south-side Physicians Hall, now long demolished. The slender, delicate tower of St Andrew's Church is a delightful feature of George Street today, rising above its four-columned portico and triangular pediment in stark contrast to some of the modern buildings and encroaching traffic around it. Outside, it lacks space to be seen at its best, but inside is another world of exquisite, tranquil beauty. Church exteriors are seen more often these days than interiors, and perhaps the public have never fully appreciated the serenity within. The interior of St Andrew's is a masterpiece of classical purity, simplicity and invention and one of the finest examples of the period in Edinburgh. It was designed by architect David Kay in collaboration with Major Andrew Fraser, which was not unusual in those days when talented, creative 'laymen' worked with a professional architect. In the case of St Andrew's it was a happy combination.

There were other incidents worthy of note as the New Town began to take shape, and one of the most important was the battle to preserve the south side of Princes Street from development. Craig, of course, had intended that it should be retained as gardens and walkways sweeping down to a canal where the railway lines run today. An alteration to the plan had allowed for a lane called St Anne's Street to be built on a steep gradient down into what is now Waverley Station from the west end of North Bridge. The council gave permission to a Mr John Hume to erect a workshop on the site providing it did not rise above Princes Street level. Residents immediately protested in despair. This was a desecration of Craig's plan, they cried. And what next? How long before the south side of Princes Street was built up solid end to end? And in spite of sweet talk from the Town Council with their visions of a majestic new Edinburgh, how long before

St Andrew's Church was the first to be built in the New Town and opened its door in 1784. Originally envisaged by James Craig for the east side of St Andrew Square the site was surreptitiously taken by Sir Laurence Dundas for his town house, now the historic headquarters of the Royal Bank of Scotland. St Andrew's Church, with its delicate spire and exquisite interior, was placed on the north side of George Street, opposite Craig's Physicians' Hall, now long gone. It merged in 1964 with St George's, the 'balancing' church in Charlotte Square, and remains a popular place of worship today.

they were plunged back to the days when the Nor' Loch was at its most pungent? A bitter campaign and legal battle ensued that eventually reached the House of Lords. Given the kind of clout Edinburgh has always been able to swing and still retains in reserve behind the scenes, the Lords wisely were persuaded that Craig's plan should remain intact.

It was an important decision for the future of Princes Street and the New Town, and it is inconceivable that it will alter now. It accounts, however, for the commanding southside position of the vast Edwardian baroque Balmoral Hotel, now revealed in pristine freshness, having emerged from the external grime of the old North British after a major refurbishment, and why other buildings like the Waverley Market remain at Princes Street level.

The fears of the New Town residents were well justified, however. St Anne's Street became the entry to a mean, scruffy area where hawkers and dealers gathered by the score, shouting their wares. Some were the legendary cries of the old street traders, which may well have been attractive singly and at a distance, but in this overcrowded bazaar-like scene, where pickpockets abounded, it was hubbub. Certainly they were not the kind of neighbours that the aspiring New Towners would have chosen. The early disregard for planning controls on Princes Street took its toll, and the fact is that in spite of its superb site Princes Street has never architecturally been as worthy as other parts of the New Town, which is particularly the case today. Nonetheless, it was clear that residents were quickly developing a sense of pride in their fine new town and they were prepared jointly to fight to ensure that its position of prestige was maintained.

The horse and cart was, of course, the principal means of load-carrying, and at the peak of the development more than 1,800 cartloads of dirt and rubble were deposited each day at the dumping ground halfway along Princes Street. It was a fascinating sight as the workmen dug at the foundations, the stones were cut and rocked into place, and the carts manoeuvred through the mud and rubble as the big Clydesdale and Shire horses strained to deliver the building materials and haul away the diggings. The whole of the New Town was alive with the sounds of jingling harnesses, trundling carts and the shouts of the carters. The stone had first to be transported from the Edinburgh quarries, and on such a hilly site some horses had to be kept in readiness to be hitched to a stuck cart to provide additional horsepower to get it rolling again.

The horses were generally well looked after and the carters tended to take affectionate pride in the strength and intelligence of their charges. There was a carter's language between man and animal that ranged from click-of-the-tongue commands and encouragement, soothing murmurs and whispers to roars of frustration when a cart became bogged down, a wheel shaft snapped or a horse moved before the cart was fully filled and half the load was again deposited on the

Taking shape . . . the detail of a painting by Alexander Nasmyth from Princes Street with the workmen on the right busy constructing William Playfair's Royal Institution, which later became the Royal Scottish Academy. The site is the foot of the Mound with the piled-up Old Town in the background. The hole in the ground is the marshy area remaining after the Nor' Loch was drained. The horse and cart was still the main load carrier and there were always spare horses to help with a particularly heavy load or when a cart became bogged.

ground. Punctuating the building-site sounds, particularly approaching that George Street ridge, were cries of 'Haud up ya black deevil, hatup, hutup, hutup!' or 'Good lad, good lad . . . woa, woa, wo-aaa ye stupit b. . . , hupback, hupback!' or 'Heid up, min, heid up, vain, vain! (left)', or 'Geedup, Tam, ye daft gowk, ye're no' deid yit!'. Many of the carters had developed their own horse language whose origins had been passed down through family generations. On winter mornings of frost the horses steamed with the exertion, but it was not long before the nosebag was out and at 'lousin' time' they could be assured of a grooming and a warm stall with feed. The harness was hung handily for the next day because, apart from the Sabbath, work was expected six days a week. It was a hard life for both beast and man, sometimes in atrocious weather, but it was also a livelihood, and without a job the all-too familiar sight of destitution in the Old Town was a recurring nightmare.

As work continued, a sharp contrast developed between the completed section in the east and the building edges to the west. Around St Andrew Square and the beginning of George Street life was suddenly sophisticated. The spacious square, the elegant surrounds, and the people of status and importance who lived there created a certain style and tone and gentility that, although present in the closes down the Royal Mile, could never be displayed to quite the same effect in that cramped environment. Now there was new awareness of rank, wealth and influence. At the other end of the unfinished George Street, however, close to the open fields and woodland, a billy-can brew-up over a building-site fire was even then an early-morning priority. A stew pot often replaced it mid-morning or at suppertime, and it was likely to contain a poached rabbit or a hare, for the snares were set in the Charlotte Square area in the evening. The cards or the pitch-and-toss coins were out as soon as the gaffer strayed, along with the drams, for gambling and heavy drinking were serious problems. Keeping alcohol off the building sites was always difficult, and staggering to work and home again was not unusual. Leggings and nicky-tams were frequently worn by the workmen during bad weather to keep the mud off their trousers, but rain or fair it was the style of the day never to be without a hat, and a great variety of headgear from tam o' shanters to tiles was always on display as the New Town rose out of the whin and rock.

One enterprising Lawnmarket clothier had been so interested in the progress of the New Town that he made stepping stones across the marshy ground that was then the drained Nor' Loch. Others caught the idea and soon a shortcut of planks, bits of wood and rocks was in place which was nicknamed 'Geordie Boyd's Mud Brig' and was used by increasing numbers of sightseers and residents. The 'bridge' was quickly engulfed, however, after Lord Provost Grieve, who lived in Hanover Street, was given permission to have the New Town's excavations dumped there, and the unsightly mound of earth began to grow to enormous proportions. New property owners strolling around the building sites, checking progress, watching that huge pile expand upwards and outwards, heard the site foremen instruct carters to 'take it to the mound' — and the name stuck. At one point the rocky brown pile was estimated to be 92 feet high at the south end and 58 feet on the Princes Street side, containing 1,305,780 cartloads or a total mass of 435,250 'cubical yards of travelled earth'. Today it is double-decker buses that navigate the Mound along with a million cars and it is graced by the classical twins of the National Gallery of Scotland and the Royal Scottish Academy at its foot and the imposing Bank of Scotland head office at its summit. It even had a winter electric blanket for a time and it remains a daily shortcut for thousands of Edinburgh citizens all following in Geordie Boyd's footsteps.

Although the building of the New Town did not take place at an orderly pace, with one street completed before moving to the next, by 1791 the progress westwards had reached Charlotte Square, the last section of Craig's plan. Princes Street and George Street had developed more or less neck and neck, while Rose Street and Queen Street were built more slowly. In spite of its excellent prospect Queen Street was still assessed as the far edge of acceptable communication with the Old Town, and progress depended on feus being sold before the houses could be built. The only public buildings at that time in the New Town were the still incomplete Register House, the Theatre Royal opposite, and the Physicians' Hall and the Assembly Rooms in George Street. None of these was given universal approval by the New Towners and the physicians were full of complaints about the internal arrangements of their hall. Most of the dwelling houses were plain in the extreme, unified and harmonious, of course, which was the desired effect, but in serried, monotonous ranks to the point of boredom, and for this reason and in the face of mounting criticism it was decided to make Charlotte Square a showpiece and hopefully to stimulate others into building with more imagination.

One of the difficulties of implementing Craig's plan was that land had to be acquired before building could proceed, and throughout the construction of the New Town this had generally been successfully achieved. When it came to building Charlotte Square, however, it was found that failure to negotiate a strip of land owned by the Earl of Moray meant that Craig's grand design would require alteration. Quite simply there was not enough space to build the balancing square to complement St Andrew Square at the other end of George Street and a crescent or circus would have to be substituted. To the purist, of course, this amounted to planning sacrilege, and had it gone ahead as the Lord Provost of the time recommended, Craig's plan would have been forever flawed. Discussions with the Earl continued, however, a solution was eventually reached, and Robert Adam was commissioned to complete the plan with style. The result, of course, is a masterpiece.

In spite of his fame south of the Border, Adam never lost his affection for his own country, and to a large extent this is demonstrated in the perfection of the north side of Charlotte Square, where nowadays the National Trust for Scotland's Georgian House stands surrounded by respectable neighbours like the Secretary of State for Scotland in Bute House and the Moderator of the General Assembly

Robert Adam — he had already found fame in London and Europe before bringing his genius to the New Town. A reputation was to be lost rather than gained with his Edinburgh involvement, but his New Town masterpieces merely enhanced it. He remains one of the most significant figures in British architecture.

of the Church of Scotland at No. 7. Adam took Craig's concept of harmony and played upon the theme to produce an exquisite, controlled design of grace and unity, with classical Corinthian pillars, balustrades, circular panels and windows, yet with the ornamentation tightly disciplined into such flowing lines and dignity that it would have fitted sympathetically into any of the finest European capitals. Yet somehow, essentially, Charlotte Square reflects Edinburgh and the aspirations

ABOVE AND OVERLEAF

Winter into spring in Charlotte Square . . . the grey sky and snow act as a foil for the fine details of Robert Adam's masterpiece on its north side. It was weather like this that had Robert Louis Stevenson cursing his city, but then spring arrives and the crocuses with it and busy people go out of their way to view the early show. Living in Charlotte Square has been a pleasure for prominent people since it was first built, Lord Cockburn being one of the first in No 14, and today that north side is the official residence of the Secretary of State for Scotland in No 6, but that is not him shovelling the snow.

of the city and the age. Adam interiors were equally celebrated, and the whole effect won him further acclaim throughout Europe.

As one councillor put it, the building of Charlotte Square was the completion of Edinburgh's great adventure, and it had finished with a flourish. Of course, the adventure was far from over, but the commissioning of that first phase of the New Town with ideals high and with all at stake, then the implementation of Craig's classic plan so expeditiously and with such style, was viewed as a

courageous and remarkable achievement and an end in itself. James Craig and Robert Adam had put their stamp on Edinburgh for ever. They set the standards of the New Town and in so doing issued a challenge to others who would follow to do better if they could. Thankfully, there were many fine architects to succeed Adam and continue to create Edinburgh's fair face. Yet it is unlikely that there will ever be anything quite on the same scale or of such importance as the original building of the New Town. In perspective, the New Town and the ancient Old Town together make Edinburgh one of the most dramatic and beautiful capital cities in the world.

CHAPTER TWO

LANDMARKS

'LIVING IN EDINBURGH there abides, above all
things, a sense of its beauty. Hill, crag, castle,
rock, blue stretch of sea, the picturesque ridge
of the Old Town, the squares and terraces of
the New — these things seen once are not to
be forgotten. The quick life of today sounding
around the relics of antiquity, and
overshadowed by the august traditions of a
Kingdom, makes residence in Edinburgh more
impressive than residence in any other British
city. I have just come in — surely it never
looked so fair before! What a poem is that
Princes Street!'

Alexander Smith (1830–1867)

LIKE all great works, James Craig's New Town was a difficult act to follow. But
the same pressures that created it also began to force its expansion. Edinburgh
was booming. The success of the New Town fuelled its development. The
population, which was about 67,000 in 1801, soared to around 136,000 in 30
years. There was a steady stream of newcomers from the Highlands and
surrounding country areas in search of work and improved wages, and the
character of employment established in Edinburgh then has largely continued to
the present day. Essentially it was not manufacturing or heavy industrial, the
emphasis being on the increasing growth and importance of business, legal,
financial and service industries, which admirably suited a city with a mounting
reputation for civilised living, a concentration of men of genius, and its own
handsome good looks.

Already the city was developing southwards, but the challenge and need was
to extend Craig's classical masterpiece northwards, westwards and to the east
where the attraction of the Calton Hill area with its stunning views was

particularly beguiling. The New Town began to grow in a series of planned developments rather than as one huge single concept, the first of these having been started by James Craig in 1775 behind and to the north-east of St Andrew Square, where the Heriot Trust feued the grassland that was to become Duke Street, Elder Street and St James Square, and to the Leith side of Broughton Street. It was a hurried, faulty step before a comprehensive plan was in place, and the control disciplines which latterly characterised the building of the first New Town were largely lacking. It took some years before this easterly section was completed in the style and elegance desired, and it could be said to include York Place, which was seen as an extension to Queen Street, Picardy Place and Leith Street, finishing with Waterloo Place, the Regent Bridge and Calton Hill area.

One of the first difficulties encountered was that the open land north of Queen Street and west of Charlotte Square, with its steep slopes and rock escarpments, was not owned by the city. Much of it belonged to the Heriot Hospital, but there were other smaller holdings involved including the estate of the Earl of Moray and the picturesque woods and fields owned by artist Sir Henry Raeburn around the tiny village of Stockbridge. With pressure mounting and in the absence of a comprehensive masterplan like Craig's, the privately-owned estates began to examine development on their own account. It was on the initiative of a former Lord Provost, David Stewart, who possessed only a handful of acres, that a joint plan was eventually submitted by William Sibbald — 'the Good Town's Superintendent of Works' — and after various discussions, modifications and the passage of years, agreement was reached in 1802 to implement a plan by Sibbald and Robert Reid down the hill from Queen Street.

In perspective, the first New Town had progressed at a commendably steady pace. The commencement of the second was even faster. A pattern had been set, and although the acclaimed George Street, Queen Street and the spacious Princes Street above its valley were not to be repeated on the same grand scale, the expanding New Town developed with grace and with those original high ideals to the fore. Not only did uniformity remain a top priority, but Sibbald and Reid's plan was so hedged around with detailed safeguards and contractual requirements, street by street, that the continuance of Edinburgh's distinguished advance was assured.

The spine of the second New Town is Great King Street. Heriot Row uphill and Fettes Row to its north side were planned to correspond with the one-sided Princes Street and Queen Street, although obviously reduced in size but nonetheless built with style and elegance. The foundations were dug in 1803, the first house to be built in this new phase was No 13 Heriot Row, and the whole street took about five years to complete. The development moved northwards and it took 12 years to build Northumberland Street and Jamaica Street, starting

Marching lamps in Heriot Row . . . this most desirable of streets is home to many of the city's leading citizens. Partly because of the neighbours and also because of its splendid outlook and state of conservation, house prices have zoomed in recent years. At the turn of the century a complete house on Heriot Row cost under £4000. Today the first £1 million house is anticipated.

in 1808; work began on Abercromby Place and Great King Street in 1814, India Street in 1819 and Royal Circus the following year, and the finishing touches were made to the last house around 1823.

By the time Northumberland Street and Cumberland Street were reached, a distinct sense of hierarchy had developed. Heriot Row was and remains a handsome

boulevard occupied by some of the most distinguished public figures in the city, but by contrast in those farthest north streets, where the artisan community set up home, the quality of style and accommodation was substantially reduced. The early feus give an indication of the social strata of New Town life being formed at the time: feus were sold in Great King Street, Drummond Place and Bellevue Crescent for seven shillings per foot in front, while Heriot Row, its future status unforeseen, Abercromby Place and Northumberland Street were five shillings. Cumberland Street, Fettes Row and Royal Circus attracted only four shillings at that time.

The opportunity for the involvement of private enterprise occurred to the west where the Earl of Moray, to a plan by Gillespie Graham, created the majestic Moray Place on an awkward, hilly site. It is interesting to speculate, however, how it might have looked had it been positioned to take fuller advantage of the clifftop upon which it is built. Moray Place faces inward rather than outward over the high natural frontage of the dramatic Water of Leith ravine and the view out across the Forth. Perhaps it was inconceivable at the time that Edinburgh would spread so far beyond the Water of Leith and that future generations would view the back vista of Moray Place on its rock in such close-up from the Dean Bridge and from so many distant vantage points. Arguably a double front would have enhanced its aspect and provided Edinburgh with a further splendid northern skyline. On the other hand, it might then have been considered too imposing, the classical effect lost in exaggeration. As it is, no one is complaining and Moray Place continues in magnificence, a glorification of all that was best during Edinburgh's golden age, the finest piece of private development in the city and, in the terminology of the estate agent, with the bonus of unrivalled views from back windows. The same thoughts could be applied to the smaller, more delicate Ainslie Place and Randolph Crescent, now regrettably taking the full onslaught of Edinburgh's crazy traffic volumes. This phase of the New Town, which also includes Great Stuart Street and Doune Terrace, was planned to link Charlotte Square to Royal Circus, but the sharp fall in height made this almost impossible to achieve.

OPPOSITE

The massive columns in the centre of St Bernard's Crescent may be architecturally overpowering for a residential development, but what a piece of one-upmanship for those who live there. Perhaps it was the shinanigans in nearby Danube Street, once the site of a celebrated Edinburgh brothel, but the attractiveness of this corner of Georgian Edinburgh is sometimes underestimated. With the blossoms out in the little garden opposite it is a delight. Sadly, the motor car has taken over here and finding a parking place becomes increasingly an achievement.

It is a birthday party in Cumberland Street and two little boys at a window celebrate with balloons in a manner that would have gladdened the heart of Robert Louis Stevenson. But in the cut-and-thrust of Edinburgh's financial world, creeping office blocks and soaring house prices are children being squeezed out of the New Town today? The refurbishments and new flats along the northern edge suggest they are staging a fightback. Oops, that's your balloon that's flown over the rooftops!

The Calton Hill area posed particular difficulties. At a time when Edinburgh's Grecian period was in full classical flight its hilly prominence was reminiscent of Athens and lent itself to all kinds of imaginative possibilities. Surrounding deep gorges and rock faces, however, particularly to the west, presented challenging construction problems. With all the dramatic potential that the Calton Hill area offered, it seems extraordinary that it was also singled out as the site for the city jail. The same perplexity that bedevils today's society over what to do and how to treat lawbreakers of every sort was also confronting the Edinburgh of 200 years ago. The squalid, cramped old jail in the Canongate had become an affront. Too

Heriot Row style . . . the height of elegance and sophistication. The plans for the Northern New Town were by Robert Reid and William Sibbald and work began on Heriot Row in 1802 and was completed within five years. Nos 1, 2 and 3, as the picture indicates, and Nos 6 and 7 retain their original fanlights, which are almost New Town symbols. The lamp-posts outside Nos 5 and 10 are also original.

many prisoners were incarcerated for relatively minor offences in insanitary, dank, disease-ridden cells, and the high ideals and stately buildings of the burgeoning new Edinburgh stood out in stark and uncomfortable contrast. One commentator at the time drew the comparison between prisoners and farm animals and concluded that horses and pigs were better off.

For years there had been protests, and as far back as 1781 Edinburgh had been empowered to build a new jail. At last, in 1790, it was mercifully decided to remove at least the 'house of correction' or Bridewell from the Canongate and site it on Calton Hill, but to delay detailed decisions for further consideration. It was indicative of the times, of course, that even the building of a new prison — and later the General Post Office — should be carried out with architectural excellence, and therefore Robert Adam was given the task. The splendid new Bridewell was completed by 1795 to a semi-circular design and it is the Governor's tower house, like a miniature castle, that is seen from Princes Street today, although the rest has long since been swept away.

One of the mysteries of the planning process still unsolved is why pressing decisions — even sometimes humanitarian ones — take so long. The debate about the size, positioning and funding of the new jail continued for years despite the suffering this caused. At one point it almost found its way to Princes Street Gardens east of the Mound. What is now assessed as one of the finest sites in Europe was regarded as having all the desirable attributes for a national institution to house Scotland's toughest criminals, except that new courts would be required to blot out the building from public gaze on Princes Street. Doubtless it would have been built in Georgian magnificence, and it was argued that if this was properly carried through, there would be no loss of amenity. Wrangling and debate dragged the issue on for a few more years until finally, in 1814, it was agreed that the new jail would be situated just to the west of the Bridewell, which had been the original suggestion more than 30 years previously.

Yet even as this classically misguided decision was taken, other eyes were scanning the building possibilities of the Calton Hill area as a whole. Whether or not this rocky spur with its sweeping panoramas was the right site for an incongruous mix of prison and quality private housing, access across the separating chasm from east Princes Street was obviously a critical problem to overcome.

In 1812 a competition was launched for what was envisaged as the biggest and most exciting development scheme in the New Town. It was planned to embrace not just Calton Hill but the entire area from the east side of Leith Walk all the way down to Leith Links. The site was regarded as having the potential to outmatch anything that had been built in the New Town up to that time. Of course, if feus were to be sold successfully, an exceptional attraction was necessary to woo prospective householders from the popular west end of town, but half a glance confirmed that Calton Hill and the approaches to Leith offered outstanding opportunities if handled sensitively.

Most of the land was owned by either Heriot's Hospital, Trinity Hospital or a Mr Allan, of Hillside, and they needed little persuading to make it available. Such a scheme on such a scale offered further opportunity to display the rich architectural talent on tap, and because reputations were to be made, 32 architects stepped forward. Among them were William Stark, James Gillespie, John Paterson, Robert Burn, William Burn, Robert Reid, Robert Brown and John Baxter, regarded as some of the leading figures in the country. Not all in the end took up the offer to submit reports, but it became clear that William Stark, architect from Drumsheugh, had considered the scheme in terms that were both comprehensive and innovative and his proposals demanded attention.

In digest, Stark was making a case to break with New Town convention and attach more importance to the contours and features of the location. He contended that even with planned uniformity like Craig's original gridiron New Town, streets and buildings should be fitted to natural contours rather than superimposed on them. Planning symmetry on paper, he believed, did not necessarily mean successful translation into stone and mortar on the ground. Natural features like slopes, trees and rocks should be respected and the plan as far as possible fitted to them. Stark did not live long enough to develop these thoughts, and eventually in 1819 his pupil, William Playfair, was asked to take over, utilising what was best from the earlier submissions and using Stark's grand concept as his guide.

Regrettably, much of the plan remained on paper. The site was just too big for completion as an entity, and as the years passed quality and ambition dwindled. Nonetheless, the Calton Hill streets are classically handsome and follow the hillside contours as Stark recommended. Royal Terrace, not completed until Queen Victoria's reign, has the distinction of being the city's longest single block of one facade which stretches for almost a quarter of a mile. It is magnificent and is divided into 17 separate segments featuring four Ionic and three Corinthian colonnades. The mews houses in the lanes behind are excellent examples of servants' quarters and stabling, which today have been turned into attractive homes. The panorama across the city is still CinemaScope although well hidden in summer behind the garden trees, thus presenting the classic environmental dilemma — trees or a view. The trees have won to Edinburgh's general advantage. Royal Terrace for a time was known as Whisky Row because it became home for many of Edinburgh's wealthy merchants who could watch their ships beating up the Forth from drawing-room windows. Saving obscuring trees in those days would not have been a priority. Regent Terrace presents Greek Doric porches and attractive iron balconies and railings, and behind these distinguished frontages delightful large gardens are alive with spring birdsong and lead up to the National Monument on Calton Hill's summit.

The development suffered because market forces could not in the end be denied. Public enthusiasm was centred on the west end and was not to be shifted. The hard-drinking fraternity of the Waterloo Hotel also did the area no favours

and were roundly condemned by the Kirk and the Capital's formidable army of matronly ladies. London Road with Hillside Crescent and the radiating Brunswick, Hillside and Wellington streets are the remnants of Playfair's design. Today they hardly boast the style and dignity intended, particularly on match days when Hibernian is entertaining a major football club at Easter Road and the trees of Royal Terrace Gardens are used for purposes other than admiration. Leopold Place remains interesting with its columned corners, and the Georgian 'bungalows' of Brunswick Place are really the third and fourth floors of the houses that have their foundations in the valley below.

Bridging the gulley between Princes Street and the Calton Hill was always going to be a tricky operation. The idea had been mooted as far back as the 1790s, but various properties had to be bought, the engineering was obviously a difficult task, and the whole scheme looked costly. It was felt, however, that progress must be made and by 1814 the necessary acts were in place. Robert Stevenson, R. L. S.'s grandfather who lived nearby at No 1 Baxter's Place, was appointed engineer and in the following year Richard Crichton, Archibald Elliot and James Gillespie presented designs. It is interesting to note that awareness of Edinburgh's environmental considerations was already finely tuned. Stevenson pointed out that the splendid views on either side of the bridge — the busy Leith Walk looking down to the Forth and its sailing ships and on the other side the fascinating guddle of houses with the Old Town rising in the background — would be lost if properties were constructed on the bridge itself. In 1816 Elliot began work with Stevenson's advice encouragingly understood and accepted.

It was a slow, stop-go process, with much haranguing over costs and even legal proceedings attached to the three properties which had been allowed on the south side of Princes Street, the site today of the Balmoral Hotel. The escalation of costs was even greater than feared and the banks were forced to mount a rescue operation. It took seven years to complete what was, in effect, a major work 50 feet above a precipice and including the Regent Bridge, Waterloo Place and a fine new post office. A simple, delicate Corinthian 'triumphal' arch is on either side of the bridge in the centre, the buildings are symmetrically classical in style, and

OPPOSITE

The noble Regent Terrace on the flank of Calton Hill remains one of the finest of the New Town developments. Unlike the rest of the New Town, which follows a square grid pattern irrespective of contour, both Regent Terrace and Carlton Terrace into Royal Terrace follow the natural shape of the slope. This innovation was the thinking of architect William Stark, although it was his pupil William Playfair who continued the work after Stark's death. Looking east the picture shows the meticulous attention to detail with fluted Greek Doric column door pieces, a fine display of ironmongery and a continuous balcony on the first floor.

where there is no room for buildings the screening walls have been made interesting by tiny columns and recesses.

It remains one of Edinburgh's pleasures to walk into the imposing Georgian post office at the east end of North Bridge and ask for a stamp. The GPO is a favourite trysting place, and its magnificence is the envy of other cities. Back in 1757 it took around 87 hours to carry the mail from London, hazarding appalling roads, floods, blizzards and the threat of robbery, but the first express stagecoach service in 1776 reduced that time by some 27 hours. At the beginning of the 1800s the Post Office staff was assessed at 35, which included management, sorters and letter-carriers, the old name for the postmen. In the early days, it was situated in Main's shop opposite the Tolbooth in the High Street, then in Post-office Close before moving to the New Town where it eventually found a permanent place on the Regent Bridge. At one point the new British royal coat of arms was torn down as being 'derogatory to the independence of Scotland'. It seems it had been wrongly quartered, either by mistake or intention, to give England precedence, and the Lord Lyon King of Arms was having none of it. The foundations of the present Post Office were laid in 1861 to a design by Robert Matheson, with Prince Albert as guest of honour in what was a major state occasion with the letter-carriers smart in their new blue uniforms.

The city was well satisfied with its 'bridge to the Calton' even though the cost exceeded James Craig's entire expenditure on laying out the first New Town. As it has turned out, however, while Robert Stevenson would have been delighted with its prospects east and west, his well-meaning plea to preserve those high, wide vistas north and south across the city to Fife and the Old Town were not so well understood by his successors. The drama has been lost with the encroachment of other, taller buildings as the top of Leith Walk developed, and it now takes a stretch of the neck to glimpse the panorama of the Forth. The bridge was officially opened on August 18, 1819 for the entry of Prince Leopold of Saxe Coburg, later King of Belgium, although it had been in use for at least a couple of years before then. One of the main new commercial features was the Waterloo Hotel, which for the first time provided Edinburgh with a tavern capable of entertaining more than fifty customers in comfort. A hundred yards away and 172 years later the new Balmoral can comfortably accommodate 450 guests for dinner. Waterloo Place is now better known for Edinburgh District Council's housing department, somewhat ironic considering the emphasis on private building at the time. A detachment of Scottish Office civil servants are also quartered there and the National Bank of Pakistan at No 19 is a development that certainly could not have been envisaged in 1819, any more than the juxtaposition of Brian Thomas's betting shop next door to the Christian Science reading room at No 15!

It is 1943, the war has taken a turn for the better and Edinburgh citizens go about their business on foot, by bicycle, horse and cart, bus and tram. It is the scene outside Register House at the east end of Princes Street. Not a uniform is to be seen. The barrage balloons are up over the Forth, Aberdeen has just had its worst air raid of the war with 98 killed, but in Europe the first day-time bombing of Berlin has commenced, the 'Dambusters' breach the Mohne and Eder dams, the Allies have landed in Sicily and the Germans lose the *Scharnhorst*. And in Edinburgh no one has thought as yet of removing the grime of ages from its buildings.

By 1890 the western New Town was in place with Shandwick Place, Atholl Crescent and Coates Crescent marking a southern boundary. When the building of Raeburn Place, Dean Street, Ann Street, St Bernard's Crescent, St Bernard's Row, Malta Terrace, Saxe Coburg Place and India Place on the beautiful Raeburn estate was completed, Edinburgh old timers shook their heads in disbelief, for only a few years earlier it had seemed inconceivable that the far country around the distant village of Stockbridge could even be part of Edinburgh. Ann Street, named after Sir Henry Raeburn's wife, is a particular delight, all the finest New Town features captured in miniature to bestow upon it the secluded, intimate character of an elegant, olde worlde village. It has been so well preserved and maintained, the informal gardens so carefully tended, that its attraction possibly now excels the original.

This phase of the New Town was over by the second half of the 1820s, but across today's two-cars-a-second divide of Queensferry Street, development progressed more slowly. The stately Melville Street, also built privately and in the grand manner but with less heavy formality than Moray Place, was completed by 1826. The surrounding streets, however, were erected at a snail's pace in comparison, partly because of the war with France, partly because they were perhaps running ahead of takers and the western access to the Old Town was still not open. Indeed, by the middle of the 19th century curlews and peewits were still nesting on the land which was later to be Chester Street, Shandwick Place, Eglinton, Grosvenor and Lansdowne Crescents, Rothesay Terrace and the other streets all the way down to Belford Road. The Melville Street area retains much of its original dignity and controlled harmony, including some particularly fine ironwork with the black-painted house railings on Melville Street itself incorporating a somewhat sinister serpent's head for its entire length. The stable and servant quarters are still in place, although most now contain tastefully converted flats with cars replacing the horses and carriages.

Rutland Street and Rutland Square are sometimes missed behind the Caledonian Hotel, but they remain true to the New Town style and were designed by Archibald Elliot in 1819 although it took 20 years before work commenced. The Learmonth estate is also part of the New Town, and is often overlooked because it is surrounded by so much open space, but it includes such distinguished landmarks as Daniel Stewart's College, built in 1853, and Fettes College, 1870, and there is linkage all the way through to Inverleith.

OPPOSITE

Melville Street was the main focus in the New Town's western development and Sir Francis Walker, the principal developer, was so pleased with his work that he built his own house there. The bronze statue of Viscount Melville, who gave it his name, was added in 1857. Several prominent figures lived there, including Patrick Fraser Tytler, the historian, and among the works penned in Melville Street was a *Life of the Admirable Crichton*. Wrought iron is one of the features of this handsome street as seen on the balconies and railings, which have a somewhat sinister snake's head.

And so the building of the New Town came to a conclusion. Although the New Town style suddenly appears in small developments in unlikely parts of the city and some people who wish to be included may argue over precise boundaries or dates, the central New Town building was over by 1840 and the remainder by 1890, for there was a dramatic slowing down after the concentrated activity of the 1820s. From start to finish it had been achieved in approximately 75 years. The makers of Edinburgh's New Town were men who cared and were caught up in the excitement of fashioning something worthy and of quality that would last. Modern comparisons are unfair, but in the main in those days they did not consider how cheaply it could be done or how quickly or how extravagant the idea. Their first consideration was how well it could be done.

In today's age when architecture is sterile and quality too often a lost cause and the inferior too easily accepted, the names of those great 18th- and 19th-century planners, engineers and artists in stone who designed and built the largest and most beautiful Georgian town in Britain should be remembered with gratitude — and regret that their genius was not more evenly spread to spill into the present age. Or would they, too, be frustrated and disabled by modern briefs? Not likely! James Craig, Robert Adam, William Playfair, Rowand Anderson, David Bryce, William Burn, Robert Brown, William Chambers, Archibald Elliot, James Gillespie Graham, Thomas Hamilton, Robert Hurd, John Lessels, Robert Lorimer, Robert Matheson, James Milne, William Mylne, William Sibbald, William Stark, Robert Stevenson, Robert Reid, David Rhind, Thomas Telford, and other formidable talents whose contribution to the New Town was on a lesser scale, are names that mean little today to the throng on Princes Street or George Street or the general New Town parade. Yet their work is all around: streets, churches, banks, hospitals, galleries, monuments, institutions, commercial offices, private houses, all memorials to them just as they are now memorials of their time.

From the outset, of course, the small detail of the overall plan, as they strove for excellence, was important. The quality of individual buildings, the creation of monuments, bridges, churches, grottos, gardens, statues, railings, the preservation of landscape and its enhancement, the adornment of their new town was significant. In all this Cockburn and Scott were two of the early driving forces, and as the New Town progressed and it was revealed what a fair city was arising, thoughts even turned to ancient Greece for further inspiration. The Napoleonic Wars were vivid in the minds of everyone, and because philosophy and literature were never more appreciated than during that golden age, the Calton Hill, reminiscent of the Acropolis, became a celebratory focus.

The first New Town adornment to be set in place was therefore the Nelson Monument. It is over 30 metres in height and built in six sections just like the

68

An unusual view from the rear of St Andrew's House on the right looking up to Calton Hill. The castle-like building in the foreground is the governor's house of the old Calton Jail, all that is left of the jail and Bridewell, which were mostly demolished in the 1930s to make way for St Andrew's House. The decision to place the jail on what is one of the finest sites in Edinburgh and so close to the city centre was always considered a gross error of judgement. The jail closed in 1925 and the last woman hanged there was Jessie Kean, the infamous baby murderess from Stockbridge. Part of the St Andrew's House tarmacadam covers the bones of several murderers. In the background are the famous landmarks of Dugald Stewart's monument on the left, the Observatory and part of the old Royal High School.

great admiral's inverted telescope. Derring-do was ever popular, and above the entrance is a carving of Admiral Don Josef de Cordova's three-deck flagship the *San Josef*, with its 112 guns, which Nelson vanquished in fine style during the Battle of St Vincent. It was designed by William Burn in 1807, and Nelson dinners were once held there, but nowadays it is mostly a tourist attraction, although it also functions as a guide to Forth shipping. Gunfire still has its significance, however, for when the One O' Clock Gun blasts from Edinburgh Castle's ramparts, flighting Princes Street pigeons and producing involuntary glances watchwards, a time-ball drops from the top of the monument as if the crackshots from a mile away had scored a direct hit. On Trafalgar Day in October

69

the appropriate flags are flown to spell out again Nelson's famous signal 'England expects that every man this day will do his duty', a constant reminder to Scotland that the great admiral's geography and history teachers should also have been fired.

The Old Observatory on the Calton Hill was built to an undistinguished design by James Craig in 1792, but the desire for something on a grander scale fell to William Playfair. The New Observatory, built at a time when Edinburgh's Grecian leanings were compelling, is cruciform, with four porticos in Roman Doric style with a high central dome. At the southern corner of the boundary wall is a monument to Playfair's uncle John, who was professor of mathematics at Edinburgh University and president of the Astronomical Association. At Playfair's suggestion Craig's Old Observatory, which was never used as such, became a fortified tower.

The noble scheme to build the National Monument to commemorate those who died in the Napoleonic Wars, along with famous Scots of the past, was a case of enthusiasm running ahead of good sense and budget. The objective to build an exact replica of the Parthenon was precisely the kind of high-ideal enterprise to catch the imagination of Sir Walter Scott. Unfortunately, it did not stir the imagination of the public, who had been encouraged to donate generously to a national subscription. The plans were by Playfair and C. R. Cockerell, and when the huge blocks of Craigleith stone arrived it took 12 horses and 70 men to drag them up the hill to the site. The king himself laid the foundation stone in 1822, which should have ensured success, but by 1830 only 12 columns had been erected. When the money ran out and it became clear that no more was forthcoming, the scaffolding was dismantled and the 'ruin' has been left like that ever since. In its day it has been called many rude names, including 'Edinburgh's Disgrace' and 'Edinburgh's Pride and Poverty', and a succession of visiting comics have given their audience a cheap laugh at its expense. Nowadays, however, most Edinburgh folk regard it with kindly affection and wonder at the foresight of those old-time marketing men who over a century-and-a-half ago gave their city an instant 'designer-ruined' Greek temple to catch the attention of the tourists. Perhaps it is as well it was never completed because in scale it would almost certainly have over-dominated the scene.

Just below, facing the Old Town, is another classical building of great beauty which no longer fulfils its intended purpose — the old Royal High School, now in the safe-keeping of the Crown Office. The 'Royal High' has played an important role in Edinburgh since the 12th century, and the flitting from its home in Infirmary Street in 1829 made one of Edinburgh's memorable occasions. The band of the 17th Lancers marched ahead, and the 700 pupils, lined up military style in classroom ranks, each with a master parading before his charges, led the

It is October 21, the anniversary of the Battle of Trafalgar and Nelson's famous signal is hoisted from his Monument to remind all Scots that England expects every man to do his duty. Below is the classically magnificent old Royal High School building that one of these days may or may not be the site of a devolved Scottish Assembly.

way to the Calton Hill and their new desks set amongst Grecian splendour. A glittering retinue of High Constables, magistrates, university professors and former distinguished pupils followed in dignified procession. In a city where schools, like the weather, remain a major topic of conversation, the ancient Royal High, now moved again to Barnton in modern surrounds, has had a special place. Some of the city's leading citizens have passed through it, including Sir Walter Scott and Alexander Graham Bell, Robert Adam, three British Lord

Chancellors — Wedderburn, Erskine and Brougham — and a vast array of prominent judges, soldiers, politicians, doctors and clergy, including a Roman Catholic Archbishop as well as an Anglican Archbishop of Canterbury. Even Edward VII studied Roman history there for a time in 1859.

The splendid new school, carved out of the Calton Hill, was designed by former pupil Thomas Hamilton, and building commenced in 1825 modelled on the Temple of Theseus in Athens. A portico is its central feature, with low colonnaded wings stretching to pilastered pavilions on either side. The strength in the retaining walls on Regent Road, with flanking porticos like small temples, creates the appropriate air of dignified serenity, the classical look and impression of a building fit to house a Scottish parliament. Such a vision remains an auld sang in Scotland. There was almost a step towards it in 1976 with a referendum for a Scottish Assembly to provide the country with a degree more governmental independence than presently exists. The old school building was made ready, a debating chamber was constructed at vast cost — even the Press seating was allocated — but the referendum was lost by default. Whether Thomas Hamilton's classic masterpiece may yet be used for its second purpose to provide a further devolutionary step in the governing of Scotland remains debatable. Present political balances suggest that it is inevitable, but blurring swirls of thick Edinburgh haar prevent a clear view at this time of what the future holds for the finest classical building to come out of Edinburgh's flirtation with Greece.

Robert Burns would certainly have had no misgivings about devolution, and almost facing the old Royal High on the other side of Regent Road is a further New Town adornment, in memory of him. This little monument is suitably in the form of a circular Corinthian temple with the roof almost an exact copy of the choragic monument of Lysicrates, but bigger. Pillars are decorated with lyres and lions' heads and it was also designed by Thomas Hamilton and fits perfectly into this Scottish Grecian landscape which gave Edinburgh the name of the 'Athens of the North'. The Burns Monument was built in 1830 and for a time housed a number of interesting Burns artefacts and memorabilia, which have now been moved for safekeeping to Edinburgh museums.

Above the Burns Monument, near the top of the stairs leading from Waterloo Place, is another small circular Grecian temple based on the Acropolis monument to Lysicrates, dedicated to the much-respected Dugald Stewart, Professor of Moral Philosophy at Edinburgh University, who also lectured in mathematics and astronomy. At that time such was the passion to build in classical beauty to adorn the city that Professor Stewart, renowned philosopher that he undoubtedly was, nonetheless seems to have become somewhat over-promoted in the monumental stakes, at least in comparison with Burns. It is in the shape of a cupola supported by nine fluted Corinthian pillars with an urn in the centre, it looks out over Princes Street and features in many of the photographs taken from the Calton Hill.

The beautification of the New Town did not rely on monuments and statues alone. As far back as David I's reign in the 12th century the king had an eye for an attractive garden and ordered that the marshland below the Castle, where at least one important joust took place, be drained and cultivated between his house on the rock and the Church of St Cuthbert. In 1460 the artificial Nor' Loch was formed by building a dam where Waverley Station stands today. What was known as the Pool was the deepest part, but the rest was a defensive eight-feet deep and a useful dunking spot for local miscreants. Length of submersion depended on gravity of crime. Witches were also ducked on their way to Castle Hill for the ritual burning, and in 1656, of the seven wizards and witches whose lives were ignorantly and cruelly taken, five were held under the Nor' Loch's murky waters until all life had gone.

With the completion of the draining of the loch around 1820 to facilitate the building of the New Town, the householders between Hanover Street and Hope Street formed themselves into the Princes Street Proprietors and took steps to secure and enhance their property. The stark valley before them was the obvious development, as others had envisaged it in the past, and the services of Scottish landscape painter James Skene were engaged to produce a design. The original idea was to create a slice of attractive, unspoilt countryside in an urban setting where the Proprietors could relax, saunter through woodland paths, sniff the caller air, but retain their exclusivity by making them private. They were prepared to pay for the privilege by investing some £7,000 for 34,000 trees, bushes and landscaped pathways on their precious eight acres. A year later only 100 trees survived and the row that followed rocked Princes Street. The wrath of the Proprietors was firmly directed at the carefree manner in which the trees had been planted. From this unpropitious start, however, the gardens grew and flourished and became the envy of all who did not possess a key. Seats and statues were frowned upon at that time as ornamental frivolities that could only detract from their pristine little wilderness below the Castle. Smoking was prohibited, games and untoward behaviour, including running, were banned, but oompah band concerts were an attraction, although absolutely never on Sundays. Access keys could be bought for £3, but when the Gardens suddenly became more crowded than desirable, an investigation discovered that an entrepreneurial blacksmith called Kelly was enjoying rich pickings from forged keys made in his Rose Street shop.

The building of the Mound divided the gardens neatly in two and both sections developed separately and in entirely different ways. The Town Corporation had purchased the East Gardens back in 1716, and after the Nor' Loch

Some use Princes Street Gardens as a country walk in town, others to rest their bunions, catch the sun, listen to the music or have a picnic — and there is always a gathering to clear up the crumbs. The dedicated seats are a feature and presented by a vast array of wellwishers from memories of Tim Wright, whose Scottish dance music was frequently heard in the Gardens, to members of the Berlin Philharmonic Orchestra or those who have simply 'left their hearts in Edinburgh'.

OPPOSITE

The year is 1984, it is Festival time and Princes Street Gardens are bathed in a heatwave. The Highland dancers have the stage, yet kilts are outnumbered by shirt-sleeve order and shorts. The towers of New College at the top of the Mound are in the background and the spire on the right is the former Highland church Tolbooth St John's. There is plenty of entertainment in Princes Street Gardens, but some prefer to soak up sun and slumber.

had been drained they were used for many years for recreation, boating, fishing for eels, curling and skating in winter. John Cleghorn leased the ground and established a nursery, which lasted until the trains came and the Edinburgh and Dunbar Railway Company began pushing southwards in 1836. Entry by then was for keyholders only, at a much reduced rate from the West Gardens, but eventually the Corporation exerted its authority and to great public acclaim the East Gardens were opened to everyone as one of the first public parks in Britain.

Pressure increased on the reluctant Proprietors to do likewise at the west end. They mounted a stalwart rearguard action to preserve their miniature Eden from the noisy, smokey trains, but the mood of the country and the need for the great railway expansion was against them. At last they agreed that the link between south and west could be forged, providing, of course, that those distasteful, clanking monsters were not visible from drawing-room windows. William Playfair was commissioned to find ways to screen the line, and few would disagree that it was another successful mission completed by him. On May 20, 1846 the first train of the North British Railway trundled along the track over what had been the old Nor' Loch. Multitudes were waiting on the North Bridge for a glimpse of the shining engine and its 20 glistening new first and second-class carriages. *The Scotsman* reported at the time that they all came from Glasgow.

When that hellfire-threatening organisation called the Scottish Association for the Suppression of Drunkenness appeared on the scene, campaigning to have the gardens opened to the public at least for Christmas and Hogmanay to keep their clients out of the dram shops, the Proprietors gave in with hardly a murmur. Princes Street was becoming increasingly commercialised, the poverty outside the New Town increasingly excruciating, the clamour to emulate the East Gardens and throw away the keys increasingly compelling. In 1876 the council took over and five years later the Gardens were thrown open to all. They soon became a popular promenade where some of the latest fashions were flaunted; flowers began to appear from 1852, then the statues and monuments, and by the beginning of the 20th century the once-wild imitation woodland had been transformed into a sophisticated ornamental garden. They still attract the crowds with concerts in the Ross Open Air Theatre along with other garden activities and continue to boast the oldest giant floral clock of its kind in the world, with some 24,000 plants in its design.

Edinburgh churches also grace the New Town as striking adornments but with added dignity and grandeur, built to impress and rivet congregations of up to 1500 within required earshot of the minister. Edinburgh has always been a churchgoing city, and although congregations have dwindled markedly in recent times, many New Town churches, with some of Scotland's finest preachers in their pulpits, continue to attract substantial congregations. Edinburgh's Sabbath face is more relaxed these days under spires and steeples that lend drama to the Edinburgh skyline or impressively catch the eye as carefully-planned elements of street punctuation.

St Andrew's Church, united with the congregation of St George's in Charlotte Square since 1964, came first. When it was opened, its six-bell peal after the English style drew opposition from New Town traditionalists who felt it should have had the full Scottish eight-bell toll. It was an aberration rectified when William Sibbald later added his steeple, and it is claimed that the ringing of St Andrew's Church bells was the inspiration behind the composition of 'Wha'll buy my caller herrin''?

St George's was originally planned by Robert Adam for Charlotte Square but was later abandoned on cost grounds and Robert Reid took over the design. Now called West Register House, its enormous Ionic columns are out of scale with the rest of the surrounding exquisiteness, but its dome is a prominent city landmark.

Playfair's unusual-looking St Stephen's Church forms an impressive end-piece at the foot of the hill leading down from Frederick Street, although some say its scale and position were determined by the Town Council getting its own back on The Edinburgh Academy by blocking out the school's view from Henderson Row, where it had been built on the site they originally selected to house the Royal High School.

St Cuthbert's in Lothian Road has changed its face many times over the centuries and twice during the New Town's period of development in 1774 and 1893. The steeple is the remaining connection with the 18th century, but the little watchtower which was built as a lookout against the body-snatchers of the 19th century, who robbed graves for medical research, has now been restored in King's Stables Road.

Broughton Place Church by Archibald Elliot and St Bernard's Church by James Milne are others built at this time which add to the dignity of the city. Sir George Scott's towering Episcopal St Mary's Cathedral at the end of Melville Street, the second largest church in Scotland, with its Mary and Barbara spires named after the Walker sisters of Coates, is not to be confused with Gillespie Graham's Roman Catholic St Mary's Metropolitan Cathedral in Broughton Street. Scottish Catholics and Episcopalians suffered under severe penal laws during much of the Georgian period, which restricted church building for them, but St John's Episcopal Chapel by William Burn at the West End of Princes Street, Elliot's St Paul's and James Adam's St George's in York Place, are worthy features which have won their places as further stately elaborations on the New Town theme.

Five years before the Royal High School moved to the Calton Hill, an

important new school opened in the New Town. Both Walter Scott and Lord Cockburn with their friend and wealthy city merchant Leonard Horner, brother of the advocate, economist and writer Francis Horner, had been pressing for an independent school with an emphasis on the classics which would give Scots the background to compete on an equal basis with England for those important government posts that seemed to be monopolised by graduates from the English public school system. It was a further example that at this time Scotland's ambitions were limitless. The Edinburgh Academy (like *The Scotsman* it always takes a capital T in the definite article, although that newspaper's main Glasgow competitor delights in always printing its rival's title in lower case) went its own way from the beginning in 1824 and remains one of the finest schools in Scotland with a proud record in academic achievement and fulfilling its aim to provide the country with many of its public figures. Even today, apart from its remarkable contribution to the Scottish bench, it numbers a string of old boy dignitaries from General Sir Philip Christison to Sir Hector Laing and to disprove the 'elitist' insult that was hurled at it when the fees were still two guineas, among its former pupils are the television personalities Magnus Magnusson, Gordon Honeycombe and the disc jockey Nicky Campbell.

With such high ideals it was no surprise that it should also look the part in Henderson Row, and William Burn was given the commission. James Grant describes the building somewhat left-handedly as a 'low and plain-looking edifice, in the Grecian style, with a pillared portico and is constructed with reference more to internal accommodation than external display'. It does not have the impact and grandness of the old Royal High School, which was of some consolation to the Town Council, because in the increasingly class-conscious Edinburgh of the time, no opportunity was lost to demonstrate its thorough disapproval of the new challenger's lofty ambitions and high fees.

The other famous New Town private schools were built much later. Fettes College is like a filmset Transylvanian palace, but in reality it is architect David Bryce in his best and most flamboyant French chateau style. Built in 1870, its tall slender spire dominates the northern Edinburgh skyline, with the new Broughton High School and police headquarters below in its shadow. It is an ornate, grand gesture of gargoyles, carved chimneys, towers and even a stone swarm of bees, which echoes the coat of arms of Sir William Fettes, who founded the school. Whatever the achievements of future pupils, they are unlikely to surpass the

OPPOSITE

It is 1976 and Edinburgh's herbaceous timepiece in West Princes Street Gardens has ticked up its century . . . it can take more than 24,000 plants and two men up to five weeks to complete the detail on the Floral Clock. It remains the oldest clock of its kind in the world.

Different fashions, different uniforms, a different gate but at first glance little else has outwardly changed at The Edinburgh Academy in Henderson Row since it was opened by Sir Walter Scott in 1824. A closer look confirms that it has expanded and modernised enormously. It was founded as a school of excellence and little has altered in that respect either. Over the years it has produced an impressive array of celebrity "old boys", including statesmen, churchmen, explorers, soldiers, artists and writers — and Robert Louis Stevenson. It is a process that continues.

exploits of its most famous son: James Bond. Fettes was Bond's fictional Edinburgh connection — until his expulsion.

On the fringes of the New Town Daniel Stewart's Hospital (College) on the Queensferry Road was designed by David Rhind in 1855 and is now Stewart's Melville College after amalgamation with Melville College in 1972 and is another stately and elaborate magnificence. The imposing John Watson's Hospital in Belford Road was a further triumph for William Burn, and although it closed as a school in 1975, it is now the ideal home for the National Gallery of Modern Art.

OPPOSITE
The majestic sweep of Bellevue Crescent with the striking St Mary's Parish Church as a focal point was commenced around 1823. Bellevue House had been the luxurious home of General Scott and, according to Lord Cockburn, was a pleasant place of woodland, bowers, summerhouses and birdsong. Today at least some trees remain as an echo of the past. To the rear there is a tennis court and some good examples of New Town gardens in an enclosed area backed by the tall flats of London Street and Scotland Street to give it a sense of community. It was part of Reid and Sibbald's northern development.

Fettes College is the extraordinary creative explosion by David Bryce, the master architectural craftsman of Victorian Scotland, an exercise in controlled energy and flamboyant gesture. It was founded as a boys' college in 1870 by Sir William Fettes, once a grocer at the top of Bailie Fyfe's Close in the High Street, who rose and rose to become Lord Provost of Edinburgh and one of the wealthiest men of his age. Today Fettes College with its splendid grounds and sports fields is famous as a boarding school for boys — and girls — and attracts pupils from around the world.

The most eye-catching of the Edinburgh adornments is the 200-foot high monument to Sir Walter Scott in East Princes Street Gardens. Some perceive it as a romantic faerie castle or as a spaceship, some consider it a Gothic monstrosity, others a magnificence. Charles Dickens thought it looked like a church spire stuck into the ground. Whatever the view, the Princes Street panorama would hardly be the same without it, and honouring Sir Walter appropriately was always going to be cause for argument. As in his life, creating his memorial never failed to produce the unexpected. Edinburgh sensibly launched an open competition to find the best design, and with 54 entries in a city renowned for its architectural genius there was considerable excitement among the professionals. When it was announced that the winner of the 50-guinea prize was the grand-sounding John Morvo, one question dominated all others. Who was John Morvo?

When it was disclosed that John Morvo was, in fact, George Meikle Kemp, the son of a Peeblesshire shepherd, an amateur and self-taught student of drawing and perspective, shock waves struck both the organising committee and the city's architect community. But the selection and decision had been made fairly and the committee stuck to it. With a fanfare fit for a monarch, on August 15, 1840, the 69th anniversary of Scott's birth, the foundation stone was officially laid in its place. In those days they believed in style and a public holiday was declared to mark the event. A vast array of dignitaries attended, a Masonic procession marched from the University, a second gathered by the Royal Scottish Academy led by dragoons, and a seven-gun salvo blasted off in Scott's honour. Sadly, George Kemp did not live to see his controversial monument completed. Returning to his Morningside home one foggy evening, he is thought to have slipped into the Union Canal and drowned.

The foundations of the Scott Monument plunge 52 feet below the level of Princes Street, and there are 287 steps to the top balcony. Graced by 64 statuettes of Scott's characters and historical figures, Sir Walter himself sits under its tall canopy in marble, a double life-size by Sir John Steell, book on knee, pencil in hand with deerhound Maida at his feet. It took six years to construct the monument at a cost of £16,000. The finishing touches were being made in 1864, but the money to pay for it hardly arrived in a flood of Scottish munificence. Despite his popularity it required the organisation of 'Scott Balls' and 'Waverley Balls' to be held throughout the country to help raise the necessary funds.

Whatever the views, the Scott Monument is a remarkable edifice. It may be incongruous in its setting, out of step at the time with the New Town's classical tradition, but in its own right it is a showpiece eye-stopper. Why was it chosen? A small rebellion perhaps against that classical tradition? Did the judges say we've had enough of the Greeks, let's have something different? Did they know no better? It would have been interesting to study the other plans, but where are they now? The Scott Monument's very difference is so much an integral part of the Edinburgh scene that it is almost as much a symbol as the Castle. Now with a face-clean it returns to its original look, but still with its pinnacle in a small cloud of controversy. Was cleaning really necessary? Should it have been left dirty? What about the cost? Sir Walter would have smiled a knowing smile because it is the kind of self-flagellatory argument that he knew so well, even in his day, in

spite of the triumphs, and seems to provide Edinburgh with a perverse painful pleasure, or else why would it be indulged?

The Royal Scottish Academy and the National Gallery at the foot of the Mound also beautify the city but in flowing Grecian Doric. They are the work of William Playfair, who was first commissioned to produce a building as home for the Society of Antiquaries, the Royal Society and the Society for the Encouragement of the Fine Arts in Scotland. The building had a further discouraging title — The Royal Institution. Now it is the Royal Scottish Academy. Playfair began his work in 1833, on the dumping ground for the excavation diggings of the New Town foundations, and therefore the building had to be erected on piles in the soft ground. The task was completed in three years, but a decade later Playfair was asked to extend it to almost double its original size. The frontage facing Princes Street was deepened with extra columns and the sides produced with the main addition at the back. It was then that Playfair added his embellishments, including sphinxes on the roof, and the large statue of Queen Victoria by Sir John Steell appeared a few years later. It was also Playfair who was wisely asked to design the National Gallery 'twin' at the rear, this time in a warm sandstone in contrast to the colder Craigleith stone of the RSA. It was necessary at this time to curve the ugly Mound road between the Old Town and the New Town to accommodate both, and now these two magnificent galleries, with the ancient Castle and fretwork skyline above, the gardens on either flank, the Scott Monument exclamation mark and the Grecian reflections on Calton Hill set the whole tone of Scotland's capital.

The galleries are halfway along Princes Street and a natural focal and meeting point which the Festival performers utilise every August in the Mound Square for impromptu street cabaret. Jazz groups get in the groove, oblivious solo musicians tootle, strum, pluck and blow, lost in their own transcendence, theatre groups yell and act out their lines in promotional vignettes, pavement artists scratch, rub and crawl to conjure crayon masterpieces among the discarded programmes and cigarette butts, painters display, jugglers, mimers, a fire-eater and inevitably pipers of varying competence skirl supported by several thousand exuberant Festival goers and fascinated local lunchtime strollers turn the Mound Square into carnival. But why should all this fun take place during the Festival period only? Apart from the winter months, why can't it spill out into the rest of

OPPOSITE

Edinburgh after dark . . . but the Scott Monument in East Princes Street Gardens remains etched against the night sky and the marble Sir Walter looks from the shadows along with Adam Black, in the foreground, former Lord Provost and Liberal M.P., to the bright lights on Princes Street and the changes wrought by almost two centuries. But would they approve?

the summer? And why after all this time should the Mound Square be left with joke street furniture?

It is a pity, too, that those lively old Sunday 'Speakers' Corner' debating sessions seem to have lost popularity. Scots have always enjoyed an argument and this was Scotland's soapbox. Perhaps some of the propositions were half-baked or daft, some a provocation, but some were logical and convincing and certainly entertaining, hard-punch politics and religion delivered with passion, or humour, or in deadly earnest. Sunday-night television did for it, of course, but there is no reason why the soapbox orators should not try their luck at other times. There can never be enough outlets for public opinion and it was free speech. After all the trouble and debate to remove the parked cars, and with so much discussion and good ideas for the development of the Mound Square, its potential remains frustratingly untapped.

The striking 136-foot sculptured Doric column of the Melville Monument in St Andrew Square is another gilding of the New Town lily, but this time modelled on Trajan's Column in Rome. It was designed by William Burn and built with donations from the Navy in 1821, although the statue of Henry Dundas, Viscount Melville, who was Treasurer of the Navy under William Pitt, was not hoisted into place until 1828. Henry Dundas had begun his career as a lawyer and was Solicitor General in his 20s, before concentrating on politics as the Member for Midlothian. In time he amassed enormous power and held many important government posts, including Home Secretary, War Secretary and First Lord of the Admiralty. His control of the electoral system in Scotland was despised by the reforming Lord Cockburn, and Melville became the butt of the wits of the day with such unofficial behind-the-back jibes as 'Harry the Ninth' and the 'Uncrowned King of Scotland'. The Melville Monument perhaps gives St Andrew Square the emphasis which fills the gap of the missing church in Craig's plan. At the time the residents were concerned that such a tall column, along with Robert Forrest's statue, might come tumbling around their ears in the first gale of winter. Robert Stevenson was consulted for a second opinion on the foundations and pronounced the stone Viscount Melville safer than some considered him to be in the flesh.

It was a time, of course, when fashion decreed great men and great deeds would be honoured with monuments and statues. The New Town is full of them. Hardly as eye-catching as the monuments to Melville and Scott perhaps, but many have their own drama, beauty and importance, and they, too, lend eloquence and atmosphere to the city. As the years have passed, more have been added, and because Edinburgh is essentially an historical and capital city, it is fortunate now to have an unrivalled collection. There is no finer platform than Princes Street Gardens, and memorials to the famous and not-so-famous who stepped briefly on

It is mid-afternoon at the foot of the Mound beside the Royal Scottish Academy and suddenly the Edinburgh mood changes. The light fades, the temperature drops and the haar sweeps in from the North Sea. In moments the Old Town skyline and Castle are obliterated, the top of the Scott Monument only a few yards away is lost. Dramatically Edinburgh is enfolded in a grey shroud. The hot dog man's stall is at once bright, cosy and inviting, but he has no takers. The green man at the busy crossing says go, but only two people are prepared to confront the haar ghosts.

the ancient Edinburgh stage or for causes lost or won are discovered unexpectedly at every turn.

Inevitably war is remembered, and those who fell, in a corner of West Princes Street Gardens, just below the hum of Mound traffic, and missed by the main drift of visitors. The Royal Scots, oldest regiment in the British Army, are remembered. Memorials are not everyone's predilection, but whether it is the peace of the spot, the sweet scent of the surrounding flowers or the timeless

George Street and ancient St Andrew's and St George's Church, once a New Town focus, is now being crowded on the pavement, its slender spire almost an exclamation mark. When George Street was first built it was the personification of genteel living and the fashion-conscious New Towners represented a daily fashion parade. In an age of casual dress the formality of the old days is still maintained Monday to Friday by the legal and business community, but try to find a suit in the hurly-burly on a Saturday morning . . .

fortress above, this tribute to the Royals is a moving, atmospheric experience. Battle honours and campaigns recite their own story: Tangier 1680, Namur, Blenheim, Ramillies, Oudenarde, Malplaquet, Louisburg, Havannah, Egmont, St Lucia, Corunna, Busaco, Salamanca, Vittoria, San Sebastian, Nive, Niagara, Waterloo, Nagpore, Maheidpoor, Ava, Alma, Inkerman, Sevastopol, Taku Forts,

Pekin, Le Cateu, Marne, Ypres, Loos, Somme, Arras, Lys, Struma, Gallipoli, Palestine, defence of Escot Odon, Aart, Plushing, campaigns throughout the Second World War, ending in Kohima, Burma . . . . and although they are not mentioned, Suez in 1956, the Gulf in 1991 and the ongoing campaign in Ulster. Wherever trouble has arisen around the world, the Royal Scots have been in the thick of it. Since 1633, when the regiment was founded, they have performed distinguished, honourable and courageous service for their country. 'Not for glory or riches', as the words from the Treaty of Arbroath, inscribed on the monument's seven plinths, remind visitors, 'neither is it for honours that we fight, but it is for the sake of liberty alone which no true man loseth but at the cost of his life.' The toll of Royal Scots over three-and-a-half centuries has been severe. The memorial to them in Princes Street Gardens, within earshot of the pipes and drums from the Castle Esplanade, is a fitting place of peace. It was unveiled by the Queen in 1952 and the low relief carvings are by C. Pilkington Jackson, the same sculptor who fashioned the equestrian statue of Robert the Bruce at Bannockburn.

A mounted Royal Scots Greys trooper in bronze, sheathed rifle on right, sabre to left, ears of horse pricking forward, breeze catching its tail, is the striking monument to those of the regiment who were lost in the Boer War. In these days of tanks and armoured vehicles the exploits of the horse soldiers tend to be forgotten, and this smart, busbied trooper taking a hard look up Frederick Street is a stirring reminder of those older days and the courage and terrible slaughter that were part of them. The Greys had their beginnings as one of the troops of Dragoons raised in 1678 by the legendary Tam Dalzell to suppress the Covenanters. When they left Edinburgh for the South African campaign, even their famous grey horses were dyed to provide maximum camouflage. It was to little avail, for the regiment had a particularly gruelling war against the Boers. The carnage among their beloved horses alone was 45,000 killed or destroyed. The Earl of Rosebery unveiled the memorial by W. Birnie Rhind in 1906 with the hope that such conflict one day would be a thing of the past. The possibility of a world war only eight years later was inconceivable. After that slaughter incredulity would have greeted the suggestion that the nations could be so demented as to go to arms again for a second world war. The Royal Scots Greys were part of both, and those who died, including some very senior ranks, are now also properly recorded on the monument.

One of the most beautiful of the war memorials in West Princes Street Gardens is 'The Call', an exquisitely sculpted young soldier, bare-headed, rifle across knee, one finger crooked into the trigger-guard in readiness, face raised in expectation, wonderfully alert, waiting . . . for what? Behind him is a 30-foot-long relief of Scotland marching to war, the pipes and drums out front, soldiers,

It is November and an old soldier pays tribute to lost comrades in the Gardens of Remembrance in Princes Street Gardens. There are several monuments in the Gardens to the fallen in campaigns around the world, including the heather garden to those who fell in the Falklands War. The monument to the Royal Scots in a peaceful corner within earshot of the pipes from the Castle above remains a fitting memorial to Britain's oldest regiment.

seamen, miners, shepherds, the Scottish people answering the call of duty of their country *in extremis*. It is the Scottish/American memorial of the First World War, the work of Dr Robert Tait McKenzie, lecturer in anatomy and head of the physical education department at Pennsylvania University. The model was one of his students, Granville Carrel. It was erected as a tribute from Americans of

Scottish blood and sympathies and bears the legend 'If it be life that waits I shall live forever unconquered in death. I shall die at last strong in my pride and free'.

A couple of strides across the path is a simple memorial in white heather to those who lost their lives in the battle for freedom in the Falkland Islands. It was dedicated on November 28, 1982 and is a replica of the heather garden planted and dedicated on the same day in the Falklands. No one likes war, and in times of peace inevitably the military become less appreciated, a recurring situation with which they have long contended. But with the first whiff of peril they are magically heroes again and the nation falls in behind them. The emotional scenes when the British forces set off for the Falklands and their return — but not all of them — will not be easily forgotten. The plaque was erected by the *Sunday Post* newspaper, a touch of sincere and fitting entrepreneurial flair, but it properly translated the wishes of the public, and without it recognition of the fallen in this most bitter conflict might have taken years.

The Norwegian Brigade are also remembered in West Princes Street Gardens in the shape of an eight-ton boulder hewn by the weather over several million years. It was erected by the Norwegian Army in 1978 to mark their 350th anniversary and in memory of the friendship and the new-found hope they discovered in Scotland after their country had been subjugated during the dark days of the 1939–1945 war. They fought bravely until they were pushed into the sea and then, like their Viking ancestors, they took to the boats in small numbers, many believing they were the only survivors, trying to reach Britain so that they could regroup to continue the fight and eventually free their country. Scotland and Norway have many close ties and a different kind of monument is set up on the Mound each December when a giant firtree is received from Bergen to sparkle out its Christmas message over the city and to symbolise a long-standing friendship.

A monument to the International Brigade was placed in East Princes Street Gardens to honour those from the Lothians and Fife who served in the Spanish Civil War between 1936 and 1939. It was a cause that created great passion at the time, a prelude to the Second World War; a million people lost their lives, but its fierce actions were overtaken and swamped in the holocaust of Hitler's war to follow. When the Edinburgh contingent of the International Brigade returned home, however, in December, 1938, they were given a hero's welcome at Waverley Station. Bands blaring, flags and banners streaming, they were marched in procession down to the Free Gardener's Hall in Picardy Place, where an emotional reception awaited with much singing of 'The Internationale' and 'The Red Flag'.

Over at the Old Calton Cemetery below the Calton Hill stands The Scottish/American Civil War memorial in red granite with a barefoot bronze slave sitting on battle flags lifting an expressively grateful right arm aloft to a rather severe-looking Abraham Lincoln. The inscription reads 'Emancipation, Education, Union, Suffrage'. Designed by American sculptor George E. Bissell, the 15-foot-high memorial, the first statue of Lincoln in Europe, was erected on a plot of land given by the Lord Provost to the American Consul at the time as a burial place for five Scottish soldiers killed in the war.

The story behind the tall obelisk in the Old Calton Cemetery is a sad reflection of its times. It commemorates the Edinburgh Society of Friends of the People, an electoral reform group founded in 1792. Its leader was Thomas Muir, a human rights' campaigner of the day, although he called it sticking up for the people. After visiting Paris at the height of the French Revolution, where he met Thomas Paine, author of *The Rights of Man*, he was seized for sedition on his return and thrown into the Tolbooth. It was feared that the Revolution would leap the Channel, and Lord Braxfield, presiding judge at the trial, took no chances that revolutionary sentiment would be heard on the streets of Edinburgh. He harshly sentenced Muir and his supporters to be transported for 14 years. The names of the friends who suffered with him are inscribed on the monument: Thomas Fyshe Palmer, William Skirving, Maurice Margarot and Joseph Gerrald. Margarot was the only one to return, but died in poverty a few years later. The foundation stone of the obelisk was laid in 1844, and in a demonstration of disgust against the unjust treatment of sincere reformers 400 members of the Complete Suffrage Association, dressed in mourning black, filed past the High Court. In his defence, Muir addressed the Court of Justiciary for three hours, and a quotation from his speech provides a telling inscription: 'I have devoted myself to the cause of the people. It is a good cause — it shall ultimately prevail — it shall finally triumph'.

Just across the road there is another of those unexpected Edinburgh monumental finds to add variety to the New Town historical scene. A bronze plaque at the foot of the Calton Hill stairs, peeping out of the ivy, is in memory of three singers who found fame in the 19th century and would have been leading attractions at the Edinburgh Festival today. John Wilson was the son of a city coachman, a printer during the week and a chorister and precentor on Sundays. As a tenor his voice was of exceptional quality and it took him to London for operatic training. Wilson's first major role was in *Guy Mannering* in Edinburgh, where he established himself in the part of Harry Bertram. He moved to live in London and became a star attraction at Covent Garden, Drury Lane and on tours throughout the world. It was while performing in Quebec that he became a victim of cholera and his career came to an abrupt conclusion in 1849. While he captivated opera lovers in London, at home his popularity was as much

Almost hidden under the ivy at the entrance to the Calton Hill at the end of Waterloo Place is the plaque commemorating three of Edinburgh's greatest singing stars who found world fame in the 19th century. Two made their names in grand opera, the other toured the world to packed audiences with a repertoire of 'auld Scots sangs'. The plaque shows John Wilson, David Kennedy and John Templeton, one-time international celebrities.

for his Scottish concerts, and it was standing room only for his 'Nicht wi' Burns' and renderings of Jacobite songs.

John Templeton's operatic career was similar and at the same period. He was from a singing family and also made his Sunday rounds of Edinburgh churches before his obvious quality demanded further training in London. Scottish tenors seem to have made their mark on the musical world, and John Templeton's two-octave range brought him Drury Lane acclaim in 1831; the celebrated Spanish opera star of her day, the great Madam Malibran, chose him as partner in her performances. He played many operatic roles, but later concentrated on concerts and like John Wilson found himself an enormous following by singing the songs of Scotland. Even in those days the glamour and tittle-tattle surrounding stage stars was a public fascination. Templeton's relationship with Madam Malibran gave the gossipmongers plenty of scope to whet the imagination. The presentation of her betrothal ring on their last performance together produced a frenzy of speculation.

The last of the singers commemorated is David Kennedy, who also began his career touring Edinburgh churches singing baritone, like his father before him as a precentor in Perth. Like Robert Wilson, Andy Stewart and Kenneth McKellar after him, he toured the world with a repertoire of 'auld Scots sangs' that brought exiles and music lovers to their feet. He played many of the leading halls in London and throughout the world and was the father of Marjory Kennedy-Fraser, the collector of Scottish folksongs who followed in his footsteps.

About this time, too, a remarkable woman called Catherine Sinclair, acting as a kind of private social worker, was hurling herself with campaigning zeal into improving the lot of the poor, whose grey faces stared from doorways across the city. The daughter of Sir John Sinclair, financier and agriculturist, Catherine set up a school to train girls for domestic service to give them a more hopeful start in life and then created a volunteer company of artisans, provided pensions for the elderly, began two 'soup kitchens', erected the first public fountain in the city, tried to improve the conditions of cabbies and even wrote successful children's stories in her spare moments. Generally she was overflowing with kind intentions and good deeds and ahead of her time. The large carved Gothic cross in her memory, like a miniature Scott Monument, by the talented David Bryce and John Rhind, is situated at the corner of North Charlotte Street and St Colme Street in the heart of the New Town.

Nearby at the Dean Bridge, that beautiful and delicate feat of engineering that spans the 106-foot chasm of the Water of Leith, another celebrity is remembered. Thomas Telford had a lifetime of bridge building and engineering before he tackled the Dean gorge at the age of 75 in 1832. It is probably his finest effort. Although thundering traffic passes across it daily as one of the main city arteries leading to the Forth Bridge, it was built more to link the expanding city than as a highway. Telford studied architecture for a time in Edinburgh while working on the New Town, and his commemorative plaque was unveiled in 1957 to mark his bicentenary. Telford was the first president of the Institution of Civil Engineers and it was this body who presented the plaque in his name.

Apart from monuments, the New Town is full of statues. Over a hundred years ago it was pointed out that Scotland's capital had many quiet corners away from the city rush which were ideal for the statues of public figures that surely would stir the thoughts of visitors more than any guide book. Edinburgh has made a noble attempt to fill many of those neuks across the years, but if fashion changes and once more statues to the famous become popular, there is plenty of room left. Naming them or knowing who they are is a frequent source of discussion for both visitors and residents. It is particularly fertile ground for pub arguments around closing time, when the innocent visitor not unfairly expects the local to have the local knowledge. As one victor succinctly put it in the vernacular after a heated disagreement in the Baillie bar over what statue directed the traffic at the intersection of George Street and Hanover Street: 'It's Geordie the Third. Ye should ken yer stookies'. In the interests of 'kenning yer stookies', the most important are as follows in the New Town.

In George Street George III does indeed stand at the junction with Hanover Street and has done so since 1831. The statue is by Sir Francis Chantrey, who also produced William Pitt the Younger at the intersection with Frederick Street two years later. The other George Street statue at the junction with Castle Street is Thomas Chalmers, the divine, who created the Free Church of Scotland following 'The Disruption'.

John Hope (1765–1823), a distinguished soldier who took over from Sir John Moore as Commander-in-Chief at Corunna and later was promoted second-in-command to Wellington himself, leans against his horse in the guise of a Roman general outside the Royal Bank of Scotland in St Andrew Square, where he became Governor. As the 4th Earl of Hopetoun and parliamentary member for Linlithgow, he was a much-respected figure in Scotland and in the British army. The bronze by Thomas Campbell was erected in 1834.

The Duke of Wellington reins in his steed outside Register House on Princes Street, and it took 30 men and eight Clydesdales to haul the 12-ton bronze into place for the public unveiling on the anniversary of the Battle of Waterloo. The 79th Highlanders and the 7th Hussars were on parade, Princes Street, Waterloo Place and North Bridge were crammed, and spectators were perched on every available rooftop, while guns on Salisbury Crags and at the Castle fired in salute. Victory over Napoleon was still fresh in many minds and the sense of relief and the success of Wellington's campaign made him a revered national hero. The statue is by Sir John Steell.

The mounted Prince Albert, in Field Marshall's uniform, another splendid piece of work in bronze by that able and prolific sculptor John Steell, is found in Charlotte Square. It has surrounding figure panels, depicting science and learning and the Army and Navy, by D. V. Stevenson and Clark Stanton. Unveiled by Queen Victoria in 1876, while the band played the chorale 'Gotha' composed by the Prince himself, it was a memorable state occasion, with the 79th Highlanders

again on ceremonial duty, the High Constables and the blue jackets from HMS *Favourite* marshalling the huge crowd — but today the statue can only be viewed from afar, locked behind Charlotte Square's railings.

Somewhat overshadowed by the Scott Monument, like all the other statues along Princes Street, missionary and explorer David Livingstone nonetheless looks ready for adventure with the good book in one hand and a large axe in the other near the entrance at the Waverley Station end of the Gardens. Livingstone was a freeman of the city, and his statue, to the design of Mrs D. O. Hill, shows him dressed for African action.

Adam Black (1784–1874) was the publisher who found success after buying the rights of the *Encyclopaedia Britannica* and some of Scott's works, then twice became Lord Provost and an Edinburgh Liberal M.P. The work of sculptor John Hutchinson, today Adam Black's statue gazes from East Princes Street Gardens into the windows of Marks and Spencer and, as one city guide jokingly remarks, if those early planners had had a little more foresight, they could have moved him a few yards eastwards so that he could look into Jenners instead.

Next to him, beside the icecream vendor in summer, is John Wilson (1785–1854), the brilliant journalist, editor, writer and acerbic who found fame and influence with the vitriol of his pen as 'Christopher North' in Blackwood's *Maga*. Appropriately, Sir John Steell has placed a well-worn stone quill in his hand. As if directed from another world in revenge for his literary maulings, Princes Street Gardens' pigeons have today responded in kind on his lofty brow from an even greater height.

At the other side of the Mound, West Princes Street Gardens is home to a number of statues like Sir John Steell's young and fit-looking Allan Ramsay (1686–1758), complete with nightcap — or at least that is how it appears as the fashion of the day. Built in Carrara marble, the statue stands above the Floral Clock and below his old 'goose pie' house in Ramsay Gardens in the Old Town, where as a publisher and bookseller he sold many of his own poems and songs from his shop, once called 'the hub of the universe'. He even founded a theatre and began the first circulating library in Scotland in Leadhills.

OPPOSITE

It is the George Street intersection with Frederick Street and William Pitt observes the changing scene as he has done since the statue was erected in 1833. In those days four lamps stood at corners of his pedestal. George Street was the pride of the New Town and was said to have no rival in the world. The Assembly Rooms ensured liveliness and at one time Edinburgh's weekly dancing assemblies had the reputation of being 'among the most brilliant and best conducted in Europe' with the ladies 'as elegant and beautiful as any in Europe'. The Assembly Rooms were also the place for banquets and public meetings. The celebration there on the return of the Black Watch in 1816 brought the city to a standstill.

Not a traffic warden in sight . . . but the Duke of Wellington appears to have the horse-drawn trams under control. The photograph was taken in 1885 and the packed tram is heading for Leith. The hoarding along its side is advertising Cod Liver Oil Emulsion. Note the small handcarts at the side of the road. The Balmoral Hotel has still to be built and the opposite side of North Bridge will see changes. Where the Carlton Hotel stands today a hoarding extols the virtues of the Great Eastern Railway below. But is there a more handsome post office anywhere in Britain?

Dr Thomas Guthrie (1803–1873) stands at Princes Street level and was depicted in Portland stone by F. W. Pomeroy in 1910. One of the leaders of the Free Church, after the Disruption, and as minister for the Free St John's kirk in the West Bow, he began his campaign for a system of Ragged Schools to give shelter, training and education to the hundreds of exploited children on the streets of Edinburgh who were in serious moral danger. One of the great preachers, he made his mark on a number of caring aspects of Edinburgh life.

The bronze Sir James Young Simpson (1811–1870) watches the passing scene at the west end of Princes Street from the Gardens. The story of how he and his assistants dramatically collapsed into slumber as they experimented in No 52 Queen Street with the anaesthetic properties of chloroform is well known. What is less appreciated is his work as one of the pioneers of modern gynaecology, and the world at the time had much to thank him for on both counts. The strong features of this remarkable doctor were caught by William Brodie in 1876.

The most recent memorial in West Princes Street Gardens has been a very long time in arriving yet is one of the most significant — to Robert Louis Stevenson. The memorial is simply a grove of young birch trees and a small, plain stone with the inscription 'A man of letters — R. L. S. — 1894'. (Do you remember in *Kidnapped* the musket balls whistling up the hillside above the birchwood of Lettermore in Appin, with the Red Fox lying dead from an assassin's bullet and Davie Balfour in hot pursuit of the man in the long dark coat, and suddenly Allan Breck was there inviting him to jouk in among the birks?). As the years pass and the young trees grow, the memorial will increase in scale and impressiveness and no doubt become a telling and fitting memorial to Edinburgh's favourite writer. The simplicity of the memorial is based on Stevenson's aversion to self-promotion, and the thinking that went into the design is by Scots poet and artist Ian Hamilton Finlay. Part of the public subscription to the Robert Louis Stevenson Memorial Appeal Fund has been donated to the alleviation of respiratory disease in children, which would have won R.L.S.'s undoubted approval.

But is this humble memorial enough? Edinburgh is the capital of Scotland, and Stevenson above all else is regarded — and regarded himself — as an Edinburgh writer. There were times when he wished he could sever the link, but whether he liked it or not, Edinburgh was part of him, and in exile his thoughts were continually dragged back to the good times in his native city. Sir Walter Scott and Robert Louis Stevenson are the greatest of Edinburgh's writers, and some would say today that R.L.S. is the more popular, yet with the spire of the Scott Monument dominating Princes Street as it reaches for the clouds only a few hundred yards away, those spindly birks are overshadowed, to say the least, and will be for years to come. In a city bristling with statues, and the latest, earmarked for the top of Leith Walk, of Sir Arthur Conan Doyle, whose links with Edinburgh were always surface-rooted, R.L.S. deserves more. In the city of Newcastle they have recently unveiled a lifesize bronze of footballer Jackie Milburn — 'War Jackie' himself, local hero — and good for them. But surely in his own city Robert Louis Stevenson, a writer fondly remembered across the world, merits as much as a soccer player?

Apart from raising the money, the main argument against erecting a statue of R.L.S. is that in all probability he would not have wanted one. It is suggested that Stevenson's opinion about statues is made bluntly clear in a letter to his lawyer friend Charles Baxter. Stevenson wrote: 'I have had a long letter from Dr Scott Dalgleish, 25 Mayfield Terrace, asking me to put my name down to the Ballantyne Memorial Committee [James Ballantyne, the publisher]. I have sent him a pretty sharp answer in favour of cutting down the memorial and giving more to the widow and children. If there is to be any foolery in the way of statues or other trash, please send them a guinea; but if they are going to take my advice and put up a simple tablet with a few heartfelt words, and really donate the bulk of the subscriptions to the wife and family, I will go to the length of twenty pounds, if you will allow me (and if the case be at all urgent); and at least I direct you to send ten pounds.'

But R.L.S. was also not without his pride or vanity and desire for recognition. His admiration for Robert Fergusson, the 'poor, white-faced, vicious boy from St Andrew's', and his fascination with the idea of Scotland's three Robbies — Robbie Burns, Robbie Fergusson and Robbie Stevenson — had him considering the idea of repairing the Fergusson stone erected by Burns in the Canongate Churchyard and rededicating it with an inscription to include his own name 'as the gift of one Edinburgh lad to another'. For all we know, as the years marched on, he might have changed his mind about statues. Or simply it might have been taken out of his hands after his death and the decision made for him without inquiring too deeply into his sentiments on the matter, which has happened often enough with public figures. The point is that for a writer of Stevenson's stature in a city that claims to nurture the arts, and which is his own city, the lack of a worthy memorial to R.L.S. is an omission.

There is also a way to correct the omission that might meet all points of view. Setting aside the question of a statue, the simplest and perhaps the most fitting way to commemorate Stevenson, and certainly the cheapest — if that is an issue — and one which R. L. S. might have approved, would be to ask the people of Edinburgh to show their appreciation by bringing a stone in that time-honoured mark of respect to build a cairn. But not just any cairn: a tall landmark cairn, a huge cairn, 100 feet high at least, placed on an appropriate vantage point so that it can be seen for miles around, a new talking point on the Edinburgh scene, for the city as well as tourists, a place to visit as a prominent and significant Edinburgh feature, somewhere high so that it can be looked up to.

It was the art historian John Ruskin who was so disgusted with the 'small, vulgar Gothic steeple' of the Scott Monument that he suggested it should be erected on Salisbury Crags. Even John Gibson Lockhart, Sir Walter Scott's biographer and one of the first editors of Blackwood's *Maga*, saw the advantage of Arthur's Seat as a site for the grand gesture and suggested that a huge Homeric cairn should be built there in memory of Scott.

Both are fitting locations for a memory of R. L. S., overlooking his city and the sea and the hills that were so important to him.

There are other sites. The Calton Hill, Stevenson's favourite stance, has plenty of room around its grassy summit. The Pentland tops of Allermuir and Caerketton, where Stevenson once expressed the wish to be buried like a Covenanter, were also favoured haunts, which would even provide that final step into the heather that from distant Vailima he thought he would never take again.

Then there is Swanston where he was happy in childhood. And in his letters he indicated a special place to Samuel Crockett, the Scots novelist: 'Do you know where the road crosses the burn under Glencorse Church? Go there and say a prayer for me: *moriturus salutat*. See that it's a sunny day; I would like it to be a Sunday . . . stand on the right hand bank just where the road goes down into the water, and shut your eyes . . .'

There would be no shortage of volunteers to build a Stevenson cairn. His old school, The Edinburgh Academy, would play a part; all schools might want to be involved; students from Edinburgh University, his university, whether or not they have tested the delights of Lothian Road or Leith Walk, could carry a stone and probably use the exercise to simultaneously raise funds for charity; colleges, companies, clubs, businesses, Scouts and Guides and families, all the Stevenson affiliations and associations, would surely want to help. If *The Scotsman* or the *Evening News* or both threw their weight behind such a plan or adopted or organised or sponsored it with an appeal to their readers — who are the people of Edinburgh and Scotland — to bring a stone to build a giant cairn for Robert Louis Stevenson, it could be achieved within a very short period. All it would then need is a stonemason to bind the rocks and surely that would not be a difficult task given the generosity of the building trade in the city in the past. Think of the publicity value for all involved.

In November 1994 it will be a century since Stevenson died. It would be appropriate if something special and imaginative and expansive were undertaken at that time. 'Robert Louis Stevenson (1850–1894). Erected in memory of R. L. S. by the citizens of Edinburgh' would not only be an appropriate inscription on a tablet but it would also fulfil Stevenson's wish that it be simple and heartfelt.

CHAPTER THREE

JUST ANOTHER FRIDAY

'AND THOU, great god of Aqua vitae!
Wha says the empire of this city,
When fou, we're sometimes capernoity:
    Be thou prepared
To hedge us frae that black banditti,
    The City Guard.'

Robert Fergusson

THE big dog fox appears out of the scrub above Regent Road, turns left along the iron railings until he catches sight of Agnes Sutherland gathering the washing from the backgreen of her house inside the Nelson Monument, then boldly steps across the grass to scavenge the remains of a baked potato beside its discarded carton. Tacking left and right to avoid groups of unseeing tourists, head and red brush held low, with quick, little, darting steps, Reynard parades towards the old Royal High School on the south side of Calton Hill and vanishes into the gorse and whin. Wow! A small boy plucks at his father's sleeve and points in disbelief, but with guidebook open his parents are absorbed in educating the rest of their yawning brood and dismiss the happening in German as merely a *hund*. Agnes Sutherland, curator of the Nelson Monument, which contains not only the New Town's highest house but also the house with the finest view in Edinburgh, collects the last of her billowing sheets, throws another glance at

OPPOSITE

It may be the Nelson Monument, but for Mrs Agnes Sutherland, custodian, it is also home. The official address is No 32 Calton Hill and from its 400-foot perch it is the house with the finest view in Edinburgh. The shape of the Monument means that when housework is involved Mrs Sutherland goes round in circles, but on a breezy day she has the fastest-drying washing in town.

Arthur's Seat, with the Moorfoots and Pentlands ranging far beyond, and closes the door to prepare tea. The tourists begin to move away, singly and by the busload because it is 5 p.m. and the inner being has also to be considered, tomorrow is Saturday and there is shopping to be completed before their journeys homeward.

Other visitors are like ants in slow motion moving across the face of Arthur's Seat, its ridges tiered in stark poster-colour contrast, vivid green where the sun falls full, dark giant shadows cast by the clouds and in the blue gullies, water-colour greys and yellows on Salisbury Crags and bleached moor, glinting light spears from St Margaret's Loch, where the tourists still linger in force. They're peching up the Radical Road, joined by early-evening fast-moving joggers, Hearts are playing Hibs in small-boy make-believe between two jackets on the green turf, John Robertson tucks away a penalty and a diminutive, disconsolate figure treks 50 yards to retrieve the mighty kick caught by the wind. A string of tankers wait their turn at anchor to unload at Hound Point as the white horses begin to buck, a flock of crows like pieces of burnt paper wheel and tumble across the sky, then dive down somewhere into Duddingston, the 17.30 King's Cross flier pulls out of Waverley Station's platform seven gently and on time and gathers pace.

Down below the New Town pubs are suddenly doing brisk business as the city's army of white-collar office staff clear their desks early with the weekend in prospect. They group by profession and social predilection: Charlotte Square young up-and-comings in Whighams and Mathers; New St Andrew's House civil servants in the Cafe Royal, along with bankers and an off-duty busker; journalists and Labour councillors halfway to the New Town in Jinglin' Geordie's; a late one or an early one in the Arts Club in Rutland Square for the literati; and more journalists in the Press Club a few doors away; soldiers in the Royal Scots Club; and office workers in general spread everywhere, natty-suited, striped and well creased.

It's standing room only in the Oxford Bar, pints of Belhaven and Caledonian downed with dedicated professionalism, and the conversation turns to former owner, Skianach Wullie Ross, aye, a true Edinburgh character, and the company lapses into anecdotal reverie. Each pub has its preferred atmosphere or slice of history or theme or decoration or barmaid or personality or beer or whisky or toastie. In the Oxford it's Ian Milne's Scottish rugby jersey hanging on the wall, in Kay's it's shiny wine kegs from its historical beginnings last century; in Milne's it's reminiscences of Hugh MacDiarmid and his clan of Scot Nats and poetic dreamings; in the Abbotsford Sir Wattie Scott holds sway, and properly so because he built the place; in the Stockbridge old Edinburgh photographs are the fascination, like the St Vincent (where, whisper it, the shotgun murder took place), but what other Edinburgh hostelry can boast a stained-glass door to the gents with the rest of its 19th-century furnishings? By six o'clock the formal suits still predominate in the Cambridge, the Shelbourne, the Baillie, the Raeburn, the Dean, Clark's and the Guildford Arms. By 6.30 they have gone, coathangered for Monday, exchanged for dinner jacket or jeans and a sweater, or gear, or studied casuals or whatever sartorial ensemble grabs their fancy as the earrings and trappings come out — for Monday is a weekend away and Friday night has still to be lived.

In Outer Edinburgh a great preparation is taking place. In Mayfield, Pilton, Porty, Musselburgh, Dalkeith, Morningside, Granton, Gorebridge, Gilmerton, Leith, Currie, Craigentinny, Corstorphine, all over the city, even in the Borders, out West and over the Forth they are getting ready to hit town. Friday night is fun night, party night, drinking night. For the young, the innocent, the hardened, the seekers of pleasure and trouble. Central Edinburgh is The Place. Eyes glisten or glint in anticipation. For them Friday night is Big Night Out, for eatin', an' boozin', an' pairtyin', discoin', an' hellraisin' — an' everythin'.

At 10 p.m. Inspector Graham Mowat addresses his Bravo Golf team from the podium in the upstairs briefing room in Gayfield police station. The night is young, like most of the bobbies who man the New Town's eight-beat night watch. With pictures of known pickpockets and car thieves glowering from the walls, the 20 or so policemen listen attentively to what they have been bequeathed from the previous shift. The atmosphere is relaxed, even jokey, but there is an understanding of what crazy Friday can conjure up, and therefore there is also an urgency to get on with the job. Five cars have already been stolen or ransacked, a 14-year-old boy is missing, counterfeit tenners and twenties are circulating in shops, the work of a true artist, and the duds are more easily dispersed among hard-pressed barmen and bleary-eyed Friday-night tipplers. The briefing takes ten minutes. Sergeant Norma Graham confirms a few details, the feet shuffle, stride down the black-and-white tiled corridor like a policeman's diced hat, and their night has begun.

A quiet, leisurely cruise along Princes Street, George Street, Queen Street, down into Stockerie and St Stephen Street and up Dundas Street tests the feel of the night. For those who can read street mood, the signs say the evening is easy, people enjoying themselves, having a good time, aggro well below the surface. But who are the baddies? Oh, they're out there, but how do you recognise them among the streetfuls of lookalikes, dressalikes, some of them clean-cut, particularly the casuals, sartorially straight from Burton's window? The cruise, a dawdling 20 mph, is a provocative brandishing of power for those who wish to see it that way: heads turn, eyes drop, avoiding contact, brakes are stood upon, not infrequently an ill-disguised V-sign is observed in the wing mirrors from the rear.

But here is a swaying youth in Rose Street, the pavement tilting below his feet, arm beckoning, waving down the patrol car in a plea for assistance. The engine ticks faster in readiness.

'Whaur's the Wine Bar, pal?' he requests good naturedly, 'I'm supposed to be meetin' friends there.'
'What time are you meeting them?'
'Ah said about half seven.'
'It's eleven.'
'Aw, it's that late. Ach, ah think a'll awa' hame then. Thanks.'
'That's a good idea. Safe journey.'

And the car eases on its way, a word with a bouncer here, a wave there, chatting up the pedestrians in friendly repartee, keeping contact, being seen, impinging gently on the city, secretly pleased that there should be no inhibition in talking to the police about the mundane.

Friday night is green baize and a flutter at the tables in Georgian magnificence at the Royal Chimes in Royal Terrace; an impromptu ceilidh singalong in the West Highland Hotel with Ian Greig on the squeeze-box; Scottish Opera or a big-name pop star at the Playhouse; a sigh of pleasured satisfaction in Rose Street's 'executive' sauna; a dress kilt dinner party at the Caledonian Club; Saturday night is pasta from the Posh Pasta Company or Cibo's or La Lanterna or the Patio or Napoli, or fancy salads in Henderson's or Szechuan and Cantonese fare in the New Sic Tek Fok or bhuna at Balli's, all in a hundred metres in Hanover Street; or up market for a sirloin from the broiler at Le Chambertin with Rainer Tenius supervising; or oysters at the Cafe Royal Oyster Bar with owner Brian Donkin asserting control; or your choice at the Caledonian Hotel presented with artistic flair and colour scheme under the gaze of head waiter George Figuerola; or Japanese or Malaysian or Turkish or Philippino or French or Moroccan or a dripping Scotch pie supper wi' saut-'n-sauce and a mealie jimmie if you fancy it.

By midnight The Venue below the Regent Bridge is fairly jumpin' wi' the racket. It looks as if the disco is on fire. Smoke drifts from door and windows, but it's stage effect only as the young ones live it up. Deafening. Assault on the lugs. Painful. Impossible even to shout with understanding. Sign language to the big bouncer with the earring and vest to come outside. Looking for a missing 14-year-old, the police explain. His photograph is on the club's identicard as a member. If he comes in, let us know.

'What do you want him for?'
'Oh, he's just missing. His mum and dad are worried. They want to know he's okay.'

'What will you do with him if he turns up?'

'We'll just make sure everything is alright. Try to get him to contact his folks. But it's up to them to sort it out together.'

'Right. If he comes in I'll ring you.'

Back at Gayfield, Constable Tom McFarlane is calling on the radio. Stabbing. In Broughton Street. Pub rammy. Four witnesses. Victim cut in leg. Assailant scarpered. Get there.

And the Astra swings round, the blue light flashes, a white-knuckle job as it arrives in under three minutes, but already another patrol car is on the spot, dealing with the situation, then ferrying the victim up to Dr Keith Little's domain in the accident unit of Edinburgh Royal Infirmary. The casualties of the night are already gathering.

The radio again. Kids running amok in gardens near the police station. Ten-year-olds. Local female resident telephoned complaint. It's 1 a.m. What on earth are ten-year-olds doing out at this hour? Screech of breaks. Norma Graham out of the car like a scalded cat. Plunges down Gayfield Place Lane, engulfed in darkness. Patrol car cuts off rear escape. Know your patch. But they've gone. Or were they ever there? Norma speaking to two bulky, homely figures eating fish suppers washed down with last of the cairry-oot. Snatch of conversation: 'Ye no feart beltin' aboot on yer ain in the dark, lass?'

More radio action: diesel being siphoned from parked lorries; girl in distress in telephone kiosk in Frederick Street; male D & I (drunk and incapable) lying in London Road, another attracting crowd in Broughton Street; bus windows smashed, fight raging on a second bus; Queen Street window stove in; suspicious occurrence in Cumberland Street, prowler reported; complaint of head-enlarging party music in St Stephen's Place; three more cars are missing.

By 2 a.m. the fringes of the New Town are asleep. Silence in a big city almost startling, darkness enveloping. But no sense of menace around Heriot Row or Moray Place, where even the birds in their gardens are at peace. Pause. No footsteps. Stillness. A car door slams in Ainslie Place like the One o' Clock Gun as a party concludes. 'Shush!' hisses a voice. In the hush the engine sparks into life with the roar of a plane in take-off. But look at the parked cars! Thousands. Who said city parking problems were caused by commuters? Number plate to number plate solid. A car thief's paradise if he could prise them apart. In the darkness Ann Street slumbers like a mystical urban Brigadoon, cars sardined on either side. 'Hope they don't get a fire here,' comment the police, 'they'll never get a fire engine between that lot.' But George Street presents an unaccustomed face, a handful of cars only, and there are more seagulls than cars, squabbling over titbits but respectfully silent. The Castle is suddenly plunged into a black void as the floodlights switch off for another night; the destination boards in Waverley Station are an unusual blank; figures sleep fitfully on bus station benches; two in a plastic sheet nest on the concrete floor; a sleepless dog-walker in slow motion on Great King Street; along Princes Street the cleansing brigade are trying to burnish Saturday's face; the Deep Sea fish bar at the top of the Walk remains busy and, yes, it is true, counting the paces, a fish supper lasts 150 metres before the remains and wrapping are deposited on London Road, Broughton Street, York Place and Leith Walk pavements.

Up at Edinburgh Royal Infirmary's accident unit the walking wounded are limping or staggering or being helped in, some by friends who can hardly stand. Cuts, bruises, sprains, broken bones and heads, some serious, mostly self-inflicted. They demand attention. 'Pronto, pronto,' shouts one at the top of his voice. On impulse another thumps the wall in drunken frustration, then his companion on the jaw and both end on the floor wrestling. A man with a slit eyebrow bangs his head against a doorway in stupified rhythm; girls sob, men swear, hurl insults, look belligerent, sorrowful, lonely, one vomits on the floor. 'Oh, God, not another blackcurrant mix,' says a disgusted nurse, 'they're the ones I can't stand!'

At 3 a.m. check all is well around the Calton Hill area, an after-dark trysting place, sinister loiterings, unsavoury beatings. Drive to the summit, headlights piercing the shadows. From on high, night-time Edinburgh is breathtakingly beautiful. A million stars in the sky and the city spread out below like a black lake, stars reflected in a million lights like the Milky Way, in clusters, strings and the black holes of Princes Street Gardens and the Castle rock, Queen Street Gardens, Leith Links, Holyrood Park, the Forth. Where Arthur's Seat was a contrast of colour in the afternoon, now it is one-tone pearl black, but its unmistakable shape is still drawn sharply against the lighter sky. Five cars are parked in isolated darkened privacy, the patrol car's headlights cutting the night like lasers, picking them out one by one, then drawing up so close to a red Volkswagen that the side mirrors almost touch. Both windows are wound down, one reluctantly.

'I hope you'll be taking your litter with you' was the Inspector's soft-voiced, unexpected comment.

'It's not ours, nothing to do with us,' said the driver, ready to argue.

'Yes, we'll pick it up. We were going to take it with us anyway,' said the passenger simultaneously.

'That's fine, then,' said the Inspector. 'A lot of tourists come up here and they don't want to see a mess. Have a good night.'

The lasers again. Three of the other cars have suddenly found business elsewhere. The headlights pick up a feeding rabbit colony, sitting tight, munching below the

National Monument, eyes ghost-like reflecting the bright beams. And, lo, remarkable, there he is, Reynard again, looking up from another discarded carton, inquisitively, moving out of vision in his own time. Who needs rabbits, perhaps he is thinking, when there's pizza aplenty.

Below among the glitter a street brawl is dispersed in York Place. A gathering of youths scatter in Lothian Road as two beat bobbies appear, a baby proclaims its unexpected early entry into the world in Comely Bank and an excited first-time dad summons police as well as ambulance; the police computer records it all: three housebreakings, a streaker in West Princes Street Gardens, more car thefts, a car race down Regent Road, a drunk driver, a car accident in Queen Street, a punch-up in Dundas Street, a dumper truck being stolen from the side of St Andrew Square, but no rush because colleagues are in attendance, all is under control.

Everything is under control, repeats the inspector, the 'all's well' report from the old city guard echoing through the centuries. Everything indeed is under control, the cost controls, efficiency controls, the utilisation of resources fine controls, the magical control of making fewer splay feet cover the same amount of territory when crime is a growth industry. The police are the guardians of the night and the night is volatile, like the day, and they must chase control — street control — move fast, impinge, organise it, manage it against the stopwatch reactions of street cries — and often screams — for help. 'If the New Town was a bucking bronco,' says one constable in graphic description, 'we're riding it hard, not coming off, winning, but sometimes we're a bit stretched.'

Now dawn is close. Friday night is over for another week. For some it has been the stuff of dreams, for others a disaster. For some joyfully life will never be quite the same again, for others it has been permanently scarred. None this night was lost. The city is still full of the homeward-bound, whizzing taxis by the convoy, groups singing, laughing, holding each other up, a few cod-eyed individuals trying to make it on their own, one depositing his liquid assets into the entrance of a George Street bank. And Jimmy the tramp is just relieved to have made it through another night.

The Gayfield duty team finish at 6 a.m., only an hour-and-a-half after the last fish supper is served in the Deep Sea round the corner. All told, it hasn't been a bad Friday night, known much worse, nothing too drastic, quite quiet in fact. Hey, but we saw a fox! Up on Calton Hill. A big one with a bushy tail. Eating pizza. Stood looking at us. Cheeky. Aye, it's not every night you see a fox in the centre of the city.

And some of us twice.

CHAPTER FOUR

MEMORIALS OF THEIR TIME

'EMBRO TOUN is me and me is it — d'ye see?
The wind will come as winds have been
But ever and aye there's us
That sits here bien and snog,
Members, son, o' an auld companie
In an auld rortie city.'

Sydney Goodsir Smith

YOU can see them silk-tied and pinstriped as they step the pavements purposefully, then vanish behind the brass-burnished plates of Adam & Co or Baillie Gifford or Union Discount or 3i's or Dundas & Wilson or Coopers & Lybrand or Stewart Ivory or a score of other financial or legal institutions on what is now James Craig's golden rectangle; or in casual elegance as they partake of afternoon tea in Jenners or Aitken & Niven or the Edinburgh Book Shop, genteel despatch-bearers of the open secrets of Heriot Row or Hart Street or Moray Place or Royal Circus, the sticky cake New Town grapevine in action; or shouting the odds in Lyon & Turnbull's auction rooms as a Bechstein goes for five grand and a plastic basin full of clothes pegs is 'given away' by Bill Plews for 50 pence; while almost next door Nick Curnow of Phillips oversees the disposal of a Sir D. Y. Cameron landscape for £5,500; or pleasurably marooned on the island bars of the Abbotsford and the Cafe Royal, contemplating the relics, listening to the table clash, how Sidney Goodsir Smith once scratched a verse on the back of a Kensitas ten-pack; or leaving ministerial affairs of state in St Andrew's House or after dispensing a five-year stretch in the High Court to airt for lunch and a read of the morning papers at the New Club; or howking the weeds in Princes Street Gardens under the watchful eyes of Andrew White and Ian Hay; or circumspectly treading the dog-walk around and around Drummond Place; or the morning meander down Dundas Street for the tweed-jacketed (blue blazers in summer)

110

pupils of The Edinburgh Academy on their way to Henderson Row; or eddying down Comely Bank Avenue, through Inverleith Park, along Raeburn Place for the boys and girls of Broughton High School; or the hesitation before ringing the doorbell of No 14 Moray Place to share a health concern with Professor Arnold Maran or Hector Chawla or their consultant colleagues, some of them the best-regarded physicians and surgeons in the world; or Danny the down-and-out sharing a shelter in Princes Street Gardens with a few of his colleagues, the shiveringest tramps in Britain as Edinburgh's east wind bites; or Moira Barnes selling Sunday papers with a smile from her makeshift stall on the pavement by Raeburn Place, where Scotland's first rugby international was played; or a sip of celebratory sherry with George Younger after completing a multi-million pound package in the head office of the Royal Bank of Scotland in St Andrew Square; or passing the round-bottomed port decanter so that it is never delayed until it reaches its starting point stand in the Bank of Scotland's eyrie atop the Mound with Bruce Puttullo presiding; or the unlikely sight down Heriot Row way of Lord Emslie, retired Lord President of the Court of Session, minus wig but dignity personified in his wellies giving the car a wash; or a uniformed lady with a yellow band to her black cap issuing instant rough justice as she solemnly posters a parking ticket on a Charlotte Square out-of-time Daimler; or the 'bowler hat' who twenty minutes later tears it off, sticks it on the car in the next space and glides away down Glenfinlas Street.

Bowlers or bunnets, pinstripes or donkey jackets, accents of the north or far south, judges or bookies or restaurateurs, bankers, builders, speculators, shopkeepers, artists, writers, broadcasters, architects, solicitors, teachers, publishers, surgeons, Chinamen, Pakistanis, ice-cream vendors, fastfood sprinters, buskers, butchers, bakers and fancy goods' makers — they all have one thing in common. They are the people of the New Town.

Most are unaware of each other's existence. Yet because the New Town still remains a big village in spite of its scurrying hordes and its importance as a centre for all kinds of Scottish institutions, there are nodding acquaintances with hundreds, good-morning-with-a-smile relationships, not always knowing who they are, except recognising familiar faces in their New Town patch and therefore neighbours acknowledged. There are obvious and clear-cut divisions among residents, of course, like the legal fraternity, the financial and architectural groupings, the long-stay residents, and for them the New Town is a rich and friendly community, where most do know each other, hold coffee and tea soirées and dinner parties together, very much like those first residents of the New Town, their distant cousins of 200 years ago. The yuppies are a small new category, young people successfully on the make and a bit flashy with it, sporting a daytime filofax and evening designer clothes, flat dwellers, living in the New

Town but disengaged and they may be gone tomorrow. In essence, New Towners are people at the very pinnacle of the Scottish social order, people who would like to be there and are endeavouring to do so, others who haven't a chance and know it, but mostly ordinary people who are content with their lot and enjoy either living there or providing a service for residents or visitors at the centre of town. They have a reasonable quality of life, brush shoulders with sirs and earls and lords and VIPs, people who make headlines or have 'good jobs', take pride in their fine surroundings, even if some find difficulty in affording them, and generally nowadays approve of the distinction of being classed a New Towner.

Today and over the centuries Edinburgh has produced citizens or attracted people who have left their stamp on history along with more than its fair share of characters, and the New Town from its beginning has been no exception. Indeed, with a resident population of around 20,000, there can be few places of similar size which, over the years, have provided so many distinguished citizens. The most fascinating insight into the early New Town is in the jottings of Lord Cockburn, a celebrated New Towner himself, who lived at 14 Charlotte Square, his winter retreat for 30 years from the country home in the fastnesses at that time of Bonaly near Colinton, and later at 2 Manor Place. A High School boy, Henry Cockburn became one of the leading figures of the Scottish Bar as well as His Majesty's Solicitor General and played a leading role in helping to fashion his city. Yet it is for his writing that he is best remembered — fascinating glimpses and overviews of contemporary Edinburgh and Scotland, sharply-drawn word pictures of friends and acquaintances, offbeat musings and personal comment gathered over a nine-year period from 1821 and published as the *Memorials Of His Time*. His experiences as a circuit judge were also published, and this wiry, witty, respected figure — 'Cocky' to his country friends — was described, according to the *Edinburgh Review*, as the 'model of a high-bred Scotch gentleman of the last distinctive school'.

Lord Cockburn wrote pungently, with shrewdness and feeling, and though a thoroughgoing Whig all his days, his writing was in the main broad-based and personal, and he was ready to give both barrels to any target that deserved it. The Town Council was such a target: '. . . omnipotent, corrupt, impenetrable. Nothing was beyond its grasp; no variety of opinion disturbed its unanimity, for the pleasure of Dundas [Henry Dundas later Lord Melville] was the sole rule for

OPPOSITE
Lord Henry Cockburn — judge, writer, social commentator, campaigner for political reform as a prominent Whig during a time of Tory domination. His off-Bench observations provide sharply-focused glimpses of New Town life in the first half of the 19th century and his promptings helped to fashion his city.

every one of them. Reporters, the fruit of free discussion, did not exist; and though they had existed, would not have dared to disclose the proceedings. Silent, powerful, submissive, mysterious, and irresponsible, they might have been sitting in Venice.' Whatever people may think of modern councillors and today's press, their healthily uneasy relationships have at least ensured more open and democratic local government.

Cockburn the countryman wrote in a different vein and with mixed feelings as he saw the green land making way for the New Town, particularly the woods around Bellevue between York Place and Canonmills: '. . . the trees were instantly cut down. They could not all have been permanently spared, but many of them might, to the comfort and adornment of future buildings . . . Trees never find favour in the sight of any Scotch mason. I remember people shuddering when they heard the axes busy in the woods and furious when they saw the bare ground. But the axes as usual triumphed'.

His similar comments on the extension of the New Town northwards of Charlotte Square provide a fascinating picture of how it all looked before the buildings and cobble setts arrived: 'It was then an open field as green turf as Scotland could boast of, with a few respectable trees on the flat, and thickly wooded on the bank along the Water of Leith . . . How glorious the prospect, on a summer evening, from Queen Street! We had got into the habit of believing that the mere charm of ground to us would keep it sacred, and were inclined to cling to our conviction even after we saw the foundations digging. We then thought with despair of our lost verdure, our banished peacefulness, our gorgeous sunsets. But it was unavoidable. We would never have got beyond the North Loch, if these feelings had been conclusive. But how can I forget the glory of that scene! on the still nights in which, with Rutherfurd, and Richardson and Jeffrey, I have stood in Queen Street, or the opening at the north-west corner of Charlotte Square, and listened to the ceaseless rural corn-craiks, nestling happily in the dewy grass.'

As the New Town developed, people began to adapt to the change of circumstances. Exclusively it was those who could afford the fine houses who made the move across the North Bridge and the trickle of the moneyed titled classes, the professional and business communities became a steady stream. Their places in the Old Town were taken over by the less well-off. It was not long before the High Street and the Canongate noticeably faded and became progressively meaner. Just as today, there were hidden costs in moving to a new development, particularly one with such ambitions, and for those on the borderline of affordability the des. res. o'er the Nor' Loch had its drawbacks. It was one thing back in the Old Town to share the same stair with nobility and wealth, sharing to some extent in their glory, but in the spread-out New Town it was a different matter. Quality of carriage and horses became important, and number of rooms and servants and furnishings. The morning coffee and afternoon tea coterie gave way to the dinner party, the dinner party became increasingly exotic and expensive — and so the time-honoured practice of keeping up with the Joneses was also as compulsive and stressful then as it is now. It was interesting how soon those who made the move began to look back from their spacious mansions to the decaying Old Town which gave them their beginnings, with affectionate nostalgia at first, then increasing incredulity that their fathers or grandfathers had lived there. It took perhaps two generations before they preferred not to think of them at all and for some even to disguise their 'land' origins.

When St Andrew Square was built it immediately became the magnet for Edinburgh's top people and, as its reputation spread, also from much further afield. In those days, partly because of communication problems but also because Edinburgh was seen as a major capital city, the desire for a town house in London was limited. Between 1778 and 1784, according to a directory compiled by Peter Williamson, a glittering array of titles, nobility, rich merchants and the legal profession were congregating in St Andrew Square. No 1 St Andrew Square, for example, was the home of the Countess of Leven; No 2 belonged to one of the heroes of Trafalgar, the Earl of Northesk, KCB, but later became a hotel; Lord Arbuthnott resided at No 5, which passed into the hands of Lord Elibank, and when he married the widow of Lord North and Grey, New Town drawing rooms gratefully received their first delectable morsel of tittle-tattle; which was as nothing to the goings-on in No 4, where the Earl of Stair, apparently tired of his beautiful wife, tried to have the marriage repudiated, so he remarried, it too broke up, he found himself back where he started and, if that were not enough to have New Town tongues clacking like steam hammers, in the background was the notorious gambler Colonel Bobadil, more commonly known to the masses as 'Bob Devil'. Edinburgh New Town society has probably never had such a toothsome scandal since.

In No 9 St Andrew Square lived Sir William Bruce; Henry, Lord Brougham and Vaux, the future Lord Chancellor, was born in No 21; Sir Patrick Murray of Ochtertyre resided in No 29 and the Earl of Wemyss in No 33. Among the heavyweights in Edinburgh's splendid square of nobility were the Countess of Errol, Lord Auchinleck, the Earls of Selkirk, Aboyne, Dalhousie and Dumfries, Lord Ankerville, Lady Betty Cunningham, Sir John Whiteford, Lord Dreghorn, Lord Methven, Sir John Colquhoun and Sir Philip Ainslie. St Andrew Square, of course, could not contain all the aristocracy who wished to share the atmosphere of gentility and civilised living that began to pervade the New Town's handsome streets. The names of the rich, titled and famous therefore began to appear throughout George Street, Queen Street and Princes Street. William Creech, the publisher of Robert Burns's first edition, lived at No 5 George Street; Burns himself was a visitor to No 25, the jolly home of James Ferrier, the Principal Clerk of Session; Sir Walter Scott's mother lived and died in No 75 and for a time Sir Walter lived at No 108; Lord Advocate Archibald Colquhoun of Killermont was in No 116 and Sir John Watson Gordon, President of the Royal Scottish Academy, in No 123.

In Queen Street No 8 was built by Chief Baron Orde of the Scottish Exchequer, a magnificent residence that was later occupied by Sir William Cunningham and later still by Sir Neil Douglas, Commander of the Forces in Scotland and Governor of Edinburgh Castle, who was wounded at Quatre Bras leading the Cameron Highlanders; the divine Henry Wellwood lived in No 13 and next door was Lord Armadale; another distinguished old soldier, General Graham Stirling, and his family lived for many years in No 27; Advocate George Paton, later Lord Justice Clerk, who created a sensation at the time by committing suicide, had his home in No 38. It was in No 52 that Professor Sir James Young Simpson conducted his dramatic experiments with chloroform which won him worldwide fame yet diminished the many other accomplishments of this remarkable doctor; No 62 belonged to Lord Jeffrey, then passed to Sir John Leslie, the son of a Largo joiner, who became Professor of Mathematics at Edinburgh University and invented the differential thermometer. 'The good Sir James' Grant resided at No 64 and in No 66 lived Professor of Law George Joseph Bell, who was the author of *Principles of the Law in Scotland*. There were, of course, many other luminaries of their day who enjoyed the quiet peace of Queen Street, which in spite of its distance from the Old Town soon became the preferred place of residence to Princes Street.

Princes Street did not get off to a good start. The attempts to build on its south side and so defeat Craig's concept of a single row of houses overlooking the Castle and the Old Town mercifully came to grief in the House of Lords after a stirring speech by Lord Mansfield. Nos 1 to 9 Princes Street, however, remained where the Balmoral Hotel stands today and this was the setting-off point for the Glasgow stagecoaches — the 'Royal Eagle' and the 'Prince Regent' — at 9 a.m. and 4 p.m. daily. Hotels also occupied the site in those early days, but No 2 had quickly been earmarked by Robertson the ladies' hairdresser.

It was in this area that the decibel count from the cries of the traders was at its highest:

> 'Haddies, caller haddies, fresh and loupin' in the creels!', shouted the fishwives with their silver-laden baskets. 'Caller partans (crabs), caller wulkes!'

> 'Braw rosy-cheekit aiples — fae the tap o' the tree, wha'll buy ma aiples!' yelled the fruit vendors.

'Wha'll buy syboes, wha'll buy neeps, wha'll buy the bonnie lass wi' the rid cheeks!' countered the vegetable sellers.

'Hot peas and beans, hot potatoes, all hot!' insisted stallholders at the top of their voices.

'Four bunches a penny, the bonny caller radishes!'

'Sonsie cheeries, ripe strawberries! Buy ma fine pears, the queens o' beauty!'

It was little wonder with such a din that the nobility did not stampede to feu property on Princes Street, and memories of the Nor' Loch stench still remained vivid. Nonetheless, some people of note did set up home and the corner house of No 27 was occupied by the Hon Henry Erskine and No 47 by Lady Gordon of Lesmore from Aberdeenshire; one of Edinburgh's worthies, the elderly Robert Craig of Riccarton, paraded Princes Street from No 91, a relic of the very old order, staff in hand, clad in giant brass-buckled shoes, knee breeches, rough-spun stockings and a hat so outrageously out of fashion that it attracted a following of small boys. No 100 was the home for many years of Lady Mary Clerk of Pennicuick (even today's Penicuik seems difficult to spell), who was known as 'The White Rose of Scotland' after a gentlemanly Macdonald during Prince Charlie's march south came upon her as a newly-born babe in Carlisle and pinned his cockade to the infant's shawl to give her family protection. Drummond of Blair Drummond was the householder of No 110 and Drummond of Gairdrum was in No 117. Sir Alexander Charles Gibson-Maitland of Clifton Hall in Lothian lived in No 129 and the celebrated Henry Siddons of the Theatre Royal 'was to be found in No 136'.

Although Princes Street was planned as a row of dignified residences, control was soon lost and as early as 1783 Poole's Coffee-house occupied No 10, which became the popular rendezvous for a somewhat discontented band of army veterans from the Indian, the Walcheren and the Peninsula campaigns. Mr Poole then turned the top half of his premises into an hotel of which his advertisements spoke most highly. No 10 also passed into the hands of famed publisher Archibald Constable.

The Royal Hotel set up business at No 53 Princes Street, and during an early outbreak of glasnost in 1817 the Grand Duke Nicholas, brother of Alexander 1, the Russian Emperor, converted it into a sumptuous suite for himself and his entourage. Baron Nicolai and Count Kutusoff, his companions, sounded as if they had just walked off the stage at the nearby Theatre Royal, but the mystery of why the Grand Duke should want to come to Edinburgh was quickly cleared up — he had been persuaded by a little-known but distinguished son of the

Lothians, a Dr Crichton, who among other things was a member of the Imperial Academy of St Petersburg and of Natural History in Moscow, a KGC of St Anne and St Vladimir and an ardent lover of Edinburgh. It is recorded that after a soldier guard from the 92nd Gordon Highlanders had been placed at the hotel the Grand Duke was so taken with the kilt and plaid that he asked if he might see the regiment — and the whole battalion was paraded before him in Princes Street for inspection. In fact, the New Town's fame had spread into Europe and a stream of prominent people 'fae foreign pairts', architects and planners came to see it for themselves.

Compared to the rest of the New Town, however, Princes Street for all its magical position did not develop with grace. That remarkable concentration of dignitaries a few hundred yards away in St Andrew Square were not impressed when Robertson the hairdresser decided to bring two Irish giants to town for exhibition at a shilling a peek from 4 p.m. until 9 p.m. except on Sundays. By all accounts they were astonishing specimens, measuring around eight feet in height and 'had the honour of being seen by their majesties and the royal family at Windsor, in 1783, with great applause . . . they excel the famous Maximilian Miller, shown in London (six feet ten); and the late Swedish giant will scarce admit comparison'. It was the days of two-headed chickens, giant rats, five-legged pigs and amazing dwarfs which were paraded as sideshows throughout the country, and like all the others the Irish giants drew the crowds amid suitable sighs of wonderment and satisfaction.

Weir's Museum was another attraction at No 16 Princes Street. It displayed an absorbing collection of 'quadrupeds, birds, fishes, insects, shells, fossils, minerals, petrifaction and anatomical preparations', and to this day Edinburgh exhibitions of remotely educational dimensions remain popular with the public. For a time the foot of the Mound became a central point for seedy sideshows, conjuring acts and puppet shows, and when the area began to fall into squalor they were at last swept away. The North British and Mercantile Insurance Company established their premises in No 64, the Tax Office was No 84 and the Osborne Hotel, which almost burned down in 1879, was No 146. In the same year two properties — No 49 and No 62 — were put up for sale at £26,000 and £24,500 respectively, which confirmed that at least commercially Princes Street was emerging as the foremost thoroughfare of its kind in Scotland.

As the houses and streets of the New Town developed to the north, east and west, so the people of title, wealth and fame, the headline-makers and opinion-formers of the age, took up residence. With them came wives, families, retinues, a new army of shopkeepers, messengers (the caddies), joiners, painters, cabbies, plumbers, all the service industries, entertainers, publicans, writers — the infrastructure of a city — and because Edinburgh has always had a talent for producing a particular strain of Capital worthy — a complex mix of brilliance, independence, pixilation and eccentricity found at all levels — the New Town was not entirely starved of citizens of character.

In the centre of the New Town during the mid-1850s the striking little figure of the Right Rev. Charles Hughes Terrot, in his knee-britches and shovel-hat, paraded Edinburgh from his front door at 19 Drummond Place as Primus of the Scottish Episcopal Church; Sir John Hope, a heroic commander in the Peninsular War, whose statue stands outside the Royal Bank of Scotland, in St Andrew Square, lived at No 57. Admiral Sir William Fairfax, flag-captain of the *Venerable* at Camperdown, was his neighbour at No 53. John Ewbank, the artist, painted many Edinburgh scenes from his home at 5 Comely Bank and latterly at 11 Howe Street; Professor John Wilson initially built his home at 6 Gloucester Place with a view to taking in lodgers, but instead it became the focus for that talented little galaxy of star writers who were the backbone of *Blackwood's Magazine*. In his garden were buried an assortment of family pets, including his dogs Rover, Bronte, Grog, Fido, Fury, Charlie, Tip and Paris, as well as a parrot. A short distance away at 1 Doune Terrace lived another publishing celebrity — Robert Chambers, who built a reputation as an historical writer as well as playing his role in the famous firm of William and Robert Chambers, who were important factors in re-establishing the Scottish identity at a time when it was in danger of being lost.

The imposing Moray Place was an obvious attraction and the Earl himself lived at No 28. The eminent legal family of Charles Hope, Lord President of the Court of Session, and his son John, who became the Lord Justice Clerk, resided at No 12. Charles Hope's exuberance to 'get at the French' saw him enlist as a private in the First Edinburgh Regiment, which he later commanded from 1801 until disbandment some 13 years later, sartorially resplendent in a swallow-tailed red coat, with white and blue facings, a fur-covered helmet with brass wings and a side hackle, white breeches, jackboots, a leopard skin saddle-cloth and a crooked sabre. Lord Francis Jeffrey, the equally imposing editor of the *Edinburgh Review*, had 24 Moray Place as his town house. Jeffrey's editorial power may have been devastating, his intellect towering, but in stature he was 'The Wee Man' to his servants and enemies, a shortcoming that gave endless delight to his friend Sydney Smith. Once Smith caught Jeffrey unawares on a donkey's back while playing with his children. Smith greeted him with a lightning verse:

> Witty as Horatius Flaccus,
> Great a Jacobin as Gracchus,
> Short, but not so fat as Bacchus,
> Riding on a little Jackass!

In Morris Street, off Moray Place, the great Thomas Chalmers D. D., leader of the Free Church, lived at No 3. Ainslie Place was the home of philosopher Dugald Stewart in No 5 and Dean Edward Ramsay, head of the Episcopal Church in Scotland, the collector of vignettes of Scottish humour and character — 'the mair kirks the mair sin' — lived at No 23. It also bristled with judges, including the distinguished scholar judge George Cranstoun, Lord Corehouse, whose title was taken from a ruined castle on the Clyde. William Ayton, Professor of Rhetoric at Edinburgh University, but better known for his writing and biting wit and as one of those spicy contributors to *Blackwood's Magazine*, lived round the corner at 16 Great Stuart Street. For years this corner of the New Town was a magnet for those who enjoyed an intellectual joust, a sophisticated dinner party and a sense of belonging to that exclusive, informal New Town club of prominent people, acceptance into whose rarified ranks depended less on who or what you were than what you were not. In many respects, after 200 years and more, not so much has altered. Judges may be fewer on the ground, the social mix somewhat diluted, the dinner party scene spread wider, but the way of life continues robust, the process of change hardly noticed as the decades slip away.

At the other end of the northern section of the New Town, people of note also set up home. It was in this area, on the north side of Picardy Place, that a group of French refugee silk weavers, after the Revocation of the Edict of Nantes, tried to grow mulberry trees on five acres of Moultray's Hill given to them in 1730. The chill breezes of Scotland's east coast were less hospitable than the warmer climes of Picardy, and inevitably nature foiled their business venture. An early resident in the new Picardy Place was Lord Eldin, one of the Clerks of Penicuik, at No 16, who was not only in the best tradition of Edinburgh judges of character, with his broad Scots accent and slight limp, but also a raconteur, master painter and wit. It is recorded that one day on the High Street he heard a young lass whisper to her companion, 'That's Johnny Clerk, the lame Lawyer'. Quickly he put the record straight. 'No madam,' he said. 'I may be a lame man, but not a lame lawyer.' His collection of paintings was famous and after his death such a large gathering arrived for the public auction that the floor gave way and around a hundred people were 'precipitated in one mass into an apartment below, filled with china and articles of vertu'. Some were seriously injured and a Mr Smith, a Moray Place banker, was found to be dead. Even then it was a big story and the talk of the town.

Sir Henry Raeburn, the celebrated painter, built a house nearby, with a gallery above and studios on the ground floor at 32 York Place, a street that became a much sought-after address. It was respectfully named for the king's second son after his English title, and Albany Street after his Scottish title. Among his neighbours were Lady Sinclair of Murkle at No 61, that giant of men

Alexander Osborne at No 40, Commissioner of the Board of Customs, who drew glances wherever he went with legs as thick as a normal person's body. As the right-hand man of the Grenadiers of the First Regiment of Royal Edinburgh Volunteers, which recruited tall men, he was presented to George III who, it is said, was astonished at his proportions. He reputedly kept in fighting trim with the consumption of nine pounds of steak at a sitting. Lord Newton at No 22 York Place had an equally prodigious propensity for claret, the tipple of the day, and three 'lang craigs' (long-necked bottles) were commonplace after dinner before indulging himself in the company of the Crochallan Fensibles until dawn, then a carriage home to York Place, a couple of hours' sleep, and he was ready again for his duties on the bench. The Queen's physician, Dr Abercrombie, lived at No 19 and Lord Craig, another writing judge, this time for the *Mirror* and *Lounger*, lived at No 10, later taken over by the dashing Admiral Sir David Milne, whose legendary exploits included the surrender to him of three French men o' war while he was still in the junior ranks and then as captain of the *Impregnable* at the attack on Algiers. In quieter vein, the painter Alexander Nasmyth lived in No 47, and it is to him and his friendship with Robert Burns that we owe the best portrait of the Bard.

The New Town was a favourite residence for artists, and William Douglas, the miniaturist, set up house in Hart Street when fame endowed him with the means to move out of his common stair flat in St James Square. George Watson, first president of the Royal Scottish Academy, lived in No 10 Forth Street, where his son also found acclaim as a portrait painter. Writer Henry Mackenzie continued his campaign against the use of Scots from No 6 Heriot Row until he was an old man, and at No 44 lived the remarkable Alison family. The Rev. Archibald Alison, it is said, from his charge in the Cowgate, was the best preacher a man could hear anywhere in the country. Such was his reputation that Constable published some of his sermons in book form. His sons, Professor Alison and the young Archibald, later an historian on the European stage and a baronet, lived in Heriot Row with him. The large house of Bellevue, which stood among woods in what is now Drummond Place Gardens, was built by General Scott of Balcomie and was a landmark for years. At one time the property had been owned by Lord Provost John Drummond and Drummond Place was named after him. General Scott, we are told, was well known for his gambling exploits, and on the news one evening during a high-stake card game that his wife had given birth to a baby girl, he decided to try to make her fortune at the table. Up went the stakes, down went his winnings until he was staring at debts of around £8,000. But the evening was still young and the bold general stuck to his task. By the end of the night his luck had turned and he drove home with a fortune of £15,000 to present to his daughter.

These are merely a few of the extraordinary range of titles and talents that peopled the early New town at its core. But the streets of the new Edinburgh, including the east and west developments, thronged with citizens of rank, influence and intellect. Scotland's capital was in the advance guard of that explosion of intellectual stimulation and exploration that encompassed the whole country at the end of the 18th century. The reasons for Scotland's flowering into its 'golden' or 'Augustan' age — more recently called the Scottish Enlightenment — have been well enough recounted, and in perspective it formed part of a European movement, but in the areas of philosophy, literature, art, architecture, mathematics, medicine, engineering, science, road and bridge building, town planning as well as other fields Scotland began to take a lead. Scots of genius like David Hume and Adam Smith, Robert Burns and Walter Scott, Ramsay and Raeburn, Adam and Playfair, Joseph Black who discovered carbon dioxide and the qualities of latent heat, William Cullen in clinical medicine, Adam Ferguson as a founder of sociology, similarly James Hutton in geology, Dugald Stewart, Thomas Reid, in aspects of philosophy, and James Watt with his steam engine were only some of the gifted freethinkers associated with this remarkable period.

One astonished English visitor observed that within a few minutes he could take 50 men of genius by the hand at the Cross in Edinburgh. Writing to a friend from his new home in St David Street, David Hume commented, 'I charge you not to think of settling in London till you have first seen our New Town which excels anything you have seen in any part of the world'. It was hardly surprising that so many important people wanted to live in Scotland's capital city and the spacious, elegant lines of the New Town along with its monuments and adornments became the stone-and-mortar symbol of the new age.

It is difficult to put a precise timescale on this dynamic period in Scottish history. Some historians maintain it began around 1730 and had reached its zenith within 60 years, but it can also be argued that it continued after Waterloo and as late as 1820 when the new and younger breed of intellectuals, with the Napoleonic wars behind them, were less moved by the arts and great works and increasingly interested in politics. What is not always appreciated is the enormous influence of Sir Walter Scott and his 'Modern Athenian' friends during this time.

Scott was the unbridled romantic, a creative genius and idealist who espoused the causes of Edinburgh and Scotland. The combined forces of his intellectual prowess, his mastery of writing and oratory, his soaring enthusiasms, his involvement and commitment helped to set Edinburgh's objectives and he also became a form of Capital quality control. Cockburn, who was on the other side of the political fence from arch Tory Walter Scott and who could not resist at times the barbed comment, nonetheless described his friend fondly: 'Scarcely even in his novels was he more striving or delightful than in society; where the halting

Sir Henry Raeburn — one of the great painting talents of the Scottish Enlightenment period. He was the poor boy from Stockbridge who became a famous portrait painter and many of the notables of his day sat for him. He amassed wealth and land and the delightful Ann Street, named after his wife, was his development with architect James Mylne. The painting above is a self portrait.

limb, the burr in the throat, the heavy cheeks, the high Goldsmith-forehead, the unkempt locks, and general plainness of appearance, with the Scotch accent and stories and sayings, all graced by gaiety, simplicity, and kindness, made a combination most worthy of being enjoyed'.

From his New Town home at 39 Castle Street outpoured some of his finest works. It was here that Scott lived and wrote for 26 years. His den was Sir Walter's secret world, the wizard's cell, where ideas tumbled headlong and his thoughts were of a thousand deeds and Scottish heroes. An original portrait of Claverhouse hung above the chimneypiece, flanked by two Highland targes and a collection of broadswords and dirks on the wall. Scott worked from a large table on which stood an old, carved box, red velvet lined, which contained ink bottles and writing equipment. A secondary desk was at its side, and apart from a few books to hand for quick reference, the rest of his library was always carefully in order: wooden blocks, named and dated, marked the place where books had been borrowed. It had a single window looking on to a patch of grass, and sometimes his dog Maida or cat Hinse would watch as the laird of No 39 scratched out his masterpieces in rapid succession.

The lameness to which Cockburn referred was the result of poliomyelitis as an infant, but as a Royal High schoolboy Scott could 'climb like a cat', as he put it, and was one of the boldest craigs-men on Salisbury Crags or the Castle rock. His writing gifts were not immediately obvious, but his legal studies at university and afterwards were punctuated by forays to the Border country where he absorbed the folklore, tales of reivers and daring adventures from an area still rich in tradition. In 1802 his first volume was published, the *Minstrelsy of the Scottish Border*, and others followed quickly: *Lay of the Last Minstrel* (1805), *Marmion* (1808), the *Lady of the Lake* (1810), *Rokeby* (1813). Edinburgh was at the height of its literary appreciation and Scott became a hero, honoured and revered. His views and comments were freely sought and just as freely given on all matters of interest to Edinburgh and Scotland, and because it was Sir Walter who gave them they immediately commanded attention. When he turned to fiction, Scott's connection with *Waverley* had not been generally revealed. After all, he was a working advocate, and at that time — and even more so today — preserving the majesty and integrity of the law was above almost all other considerations. Any member of its ranks who could be construed as bringing it into disrepute was not easily tolerated. Poetry and history were acceptable for an advocate, fiction debatable, but when Scott announced his authorship in the Assembly Rooms the outcome was sensational. The tales were so well received, the content so acceptable, the writing so admirable, the sentiments so appropriate for the times that he was hurled into a further orbit of acclaim.

They were exciting times. A publishing bonanza was taking place in the city, critical journalism was at its most cutting, worthy tomes of erudition enhanced the good name of Edinburgh as a European publishing centre of merit, and such generous rewards were paid that writers of today only wish they would return. A short walk from Castle Street brought Scott to Constables, that most eminent publishing house at No 10 Princes Street. Archibald Constable had moved his business from the Old Town in 1822 and his premises were regarded as one of the finest in Edinburgh. Constable himself was a highly regarded New Town businessman, and as a publisher at a time of literary explosion he enjoyed a reflected glory. One of his publications was the *Edinburgh Review*, a Whig-biased paper launched in 1802 by the Anglican chaplain Sydney Smith and three exceedingly committed advocates, Henry Brougham, Francis Horner and the man with the scalpel pen who became its editor, Francis Jeffrey, later Lord Advocate. It was immediately a success, much of it based on the toughness of its literary criticism which speedily developed into ferocity. Scott was pleased to contribute to such a talked-about journal until Jeffrey savaged *Marmion* in a 35-page review that reproached Scott for continuing 'such an idle task' as writing about romance and chivalry.

Inevitably a political counterbalance had to be found. The Tory *Quarterly Review* from London publisher John Murray was no match for the intellectually heavyweight Jeffrey, but then on to the New Town scene arrived the shrewd and experienced publisher William Blackwood, who set up office at No 17 Princes Street. His *Blackwood's Magazine*, ostensibly backing the Tories, stuttered at its launch, but the editors were fired, John Wilson (Scott's son-in law from 1820) and John Gibson Lockhart were engaged and, supported by James Hogg, the 'Ettrick Shepherd', to provide professional status, it became an overnight if outrageous success. With shades of some tabloid journalism today, *Blackwood's*, or *Maga* as it became popularly known, set out to outgun its competitor. Hype and hyperbole were its currency, and what they did not know or could not prove was invented.

They even trotted out the scurrilous 'Chaldee Manuscript', a mock biblical tale that was unashamedly the vehicle for scandalous personal abuse of notable people, not only rival Whigs but also confused Tories. The package included vitriolic literary criticism, and the comments by Christopher North (John Wilson) became required reading. It was deliciously disgraceful and deplorable and it sold like hot cakes. Not for the last time it was found that the public love to be titillated. The whiff of scandal, the grinding sound of gnashing teeth as the insults fly, slur, innuendo and ridicule remain a proven formula for selling some newspapers, magazines and books — if they can get away with it. Perhaps the best that could be said of both the *Edinburgh Review* and *Blackwood's* in those days was that the formula was perpetrated brilliantly. The worst that can be said is that the destructive critical analysis was in the end counterproductive, because what young writer would ever want to be submitted to such an inquisition?

Perhaps the biggest sensation of the time, however, was the dramatic collapse of Constable's publishing company in 1826, which had appeared as solid as the Castle rock. It was hardly believable. When it became known that the liabilities were spectacular and that, tragically, Sir Walter Scott was also involved, Edinburgh was stunned. He had been associated with both Constables and Ballantyne & Co, which also failed in the crash, and Scott's own share of indebtedness amounted to some £120,000, a fortune vanished. The story of how the great writer dedicated himself to literally write off his debts with his 'right hand' is well enough known, the distress of his friends who wanted to help but were confronted by Scott's implacable pride and sense of responsibility, the sad parting from No 39 Castle Street — 'it has sheltered me from the prime of life to its decline' — the miserable lodgings, the departure finally to Abbotsford, failing health, and then, at last, the great news was delivered — Scott had cleared his debts. It was the stuff itself of a novel.

Literary figures have peopled the New Town's story. Henry Mackenzie, editor of the important but unsuccessful review magazines the *Mirror* and the *Lounger*, but better known for his sentimental novel *The Man of Feeling*, moved throughout the early New Town with his fashionable obsession that writing in Scots was to be shunned. The arguments carried little weight with Robert Fergusson, the tragic young poet who died in the Edinburgh bedlam at the age of 24. Fergusson watched the New Town develop from across the Nor' Loch and he had plenty to say about the good and the flawed and he said it in Scots. Although his poetic career was so brief, Fergusson's influence on others to follow was marked, including Robert Burns, who stayed for a time in the common stair of No 2 St James Square (later renumbered 30) in the New Town. Indeed, when Burns discovered that Fergusson's remains lay in an unmarked, neglected grave in the Canongate kirkyard, he commissioned a headstone and paid for it out of his own pocket.

Since the Union of Parliaments in 1707 the trend had been to belittle the Scots language. It was viewed as uncouth, unfit for serious writing or the muse. Some of the literati still referred to Scotland as North Britain. They aped English customs and manners, decried Scottish origins, Scottish culture and national pride. Even David Hume in his New Town home felt somehow that his native tongue was inferior. Hints of Scotticisms were painstakingly edited out of his text to ensure its purity. But even Mackenzie and the henchmen who vilified Scotland recognised the genius in Burns's vernacular.

Burns's fame had preceded his Edinburgh arrival, and from the outset his message was clear-cut: pride in the Scots language, pride in Scottish traditions,

Robert Burns — the Bard lived for a time in the now demolished St James Square, just behind St Andrew Square. The unfinished portrait is by Alexander Nasmyth, another New Town resident who had his home at 47 York Place. The Nasmyth is regarded as one of the best likenesses of Scotland's greatest poet. His Edinburgh poem to Clarinda is regarded as the finest love poem ever written.

pride in Scotland and its people. It was precisely what the vast majority of Edinburgh folk and the rest of Scotland wanted to hear. At first Burns's company was sought as a curiosity, the scrutiny of a small phenomenon, an 'original' ploughman poet. Inevitably there were those who saw only the country dress, heard only the speech of Ayrshire, the stories of his tavern carousing, his encounters with the lasses. There were also those who treated both Burns the poet and Burns the man with the serious respect both demanded. It was his dignity and lack of pretension that first won regard. His conversation and power of intellect surprised and impressed the Edinburgh establishment. Burns may have been a drawing-room distraction, but Edinburgh society life was also new to him and in turn he observed it with fascination. According to his own measure of people he placed them in their stalls. And the poet in him stored it all away. The Earl of Glencairn was the first of the nobility to befriend Burns, Dugald Stewart walked with him over the Braid Hills and was filled with admiration, Lord Monboddo, Hugh Blair, Dr Adamson, Dr Blacklock and many other prominent people gave him support. They were relationships Burns valued; he felt honoured to be accepted in such discerning company; he returned their respect; but he neither boasted of their friendship, which he might have done, nor put undue stress upon it. Burns's St James Square house, which he shared with high school teacher Willie Cruikshank, is described by Robert Chambers as being composed of two upper rooms of a lofty building in an airy situation . The Poet's room had a window overlooking the garden behind Register House as well as the street entering the square. And it was here he met Clarinda.

Burns's fall from popularity in Edinburgh was dramatic and self-inflicted. Ever ready for a morsel of tittle-tattle, Edinburgh society was provided by him with a feast. His drinking bouts with new-found cronies were the talk of the town, and invitations to dine out and meet people of standing and influence became fewer. His romance with Agnes McLehose, who was a niece of Court of Session judge Lord Craig and had been deserted by her husband, created more scandal. Burns's Edinburgh days — and nights — may not have been spent wisely, but during his stay he wrote two of his best-remembered poems: 'Address to a Haggis' is full of fun and is recited with gusto at every Burns Supper throughout the world. In contrast, 'Ae Fond Kiss', his parting poem to Clarinda, the secret name for Agnes McLehose, has been called the finest love poem ever penned.

Half a century later, from an entirely different background but with the same seeds of genius and capacity to be misunderstood, Robert Louis Stevenson was born at 8 Howard Place on the northern edge of the New Town in 1850. That long, angular face with the gentle smile, dark eyes and the downward-trailing moustache was once almost a symbol portrait for Edinburgh. Being hunted across the Highlands with Allan Breck and Davie Balfour or searching for pirates' treasure with Jim Hawkins and the sinister but somehow likeable one-legged sea cook John Silver, along with those wonderful poems of childhood from the Land of Counterpane, made R. L. S. required reading in Scottish schools. Alas, that is no longer the case, and more's the pity, as Alan might have said, although the magic of the tales and the vividness of the characters have never altered.

No-one could tell a story better than Robert Louis Stevenson, and no-one has written from the inside about Scotland's contradictory capital with such knowledge and understanding. Edinburgh's own story, its sweeping vistas, the ancient castle, the distant Pentlands, the skyscrapers of the Old Town, the closes and howffs, the people of his 'precipitous city', even those on the fringes of Edinburgh's 'underworld', a term more to do then with poverty than stepping beyond the law, all the sounds and smells and clash of Edinburgh were an exciting daily performance that set his imagination flighting. R.L.S. felt Edinburgh. His interest had been well stocked since childhood by tales of adventure and the Covenanters, recounted by Alison Cunningham, his nurse — the beloved Cummy — during those long nights when the sleepless, sickly little boy waited for dawn and another sickly day.

The Stevenson household was typically professional, well-to-do New Town Edinburgh. Thomas Stevenson was an industrious father, reserved and shy, inflexibly Presbyterian, but a good man, caring deeply for his only child; his mother was a daughter of the manse with that kind of inner conviction about life's purpose that enabled her to face up stalwartly to life's tribulations; the influential Cummy, a Fifer of character, was typical of the children's nurse of the day — unattached except for her charge, a sniff of Calvinistic brimstone where she stepped, loyal, caring and very much one of the family, who would ensure her opinion was heard. It was in this environment that R.L.S. enjoyed a happy childhood, if dogged by ill health, first in Howard Place, then at 1 Inverleith Terrace (now No 9), and finally at 17 Heriot Row with interludes at their country house at Swanston.

Yet in spite of Stevenson's love affair with Edinburgh and his warm family ties, his relationships with both grew brittle. The chill of Edinburgh winters sought out the weaknesses in his chest, sapping his strength; the comfortable orderliness of New Town Victorian society and its starchy smugness was something for him to rebel against; the howffs of Leith Walk, the Old Town, Lothian Road and the folk who frequented them — who remain today an integral part of the Edinburgh schizophrenic double-act — beckoned him and he discovered solace and pleasure in their companionship; and they accepted him,

although he could only ever be an outsider, at the heart of their company but not of it. Like everything Stevenson did, he lived the experience to the hilt, which was one of his most appealing qualities.

As with so many families, it was during adolescence and student days that R.L.S.'s interests and new values clashed harshly with the other members in No 17. His revolt was against Victorian society, the stuffy conventions, the New Town's prim, unquestioning acceptance of them. Youthful affectations of manners and dress, including the celebrated velvet jacket, the fascination of those twilight denizens of the Calton Hill howffs, the bawdy, gas-lit taverns on the downhill road to Leith, his freethinking unconventionality, were the outward signals of rebellion. Both Stevenson and his family, because of their very closeness, tried to stand back from the confrontation that could only bring hurt to all. When it became clear he would not follow into the family marine engineering business, as was expected of him, the decision was therefore accepted, but with disquiet; a safe and respectable compromise was agreed that he would study law and put up his own advocate's plate, but R.L.S.'s heart was never in it, although he qualified. Still unsure of his gift, fumbling for expression, he turned towards a literary career, which had been tugging at him all the time, the joy of words and meaning, plots and characters, prose and poetry, and he had so much to say, so much life and feeling and of himself to give.

It was R.L.S.'s flirtations with atheism that brought matters to a head in the Stevenson family. Thomas Stevenson could not have taken it harder. He regarded it as the spurning of everything he and his wife and friends believed in. Anger, resentment, shame, failure, even fear for his son's salvation were all present in that upstairs room at 17 Heriot Row where the 'blasphemy' forced the confrontation. Thomas Stevenson was blunt, interrogating for the truth at last. R.L.S.'s most recent illness had left him sick of the half-truths that so often previously had circumvented the collision. He answered his father's questions frankly and honestly. 'My dear papa was in the devil of a taking . . . the thunder-bolt has fallen with a vengeance now . . .', wrote R.L.S. to his lawyer friend Charles Baxter. '. . . If I had seen the real hell of everything since I think I should have lied . . . but am I to live my whole life as one falsehood? . . . They don't see either that my game is not the light-hearted scoffer . . . I am, I think, as honest as they are in what I hold. I have not come hastily to my views . . . What a curse I am

OPPOSITE
Robert Louis Stevenson — Edinburgh's favourite son had three addresses in the New Town but 17 Heriot Row is regarded as home. R.L.S.'s relationship with his city was always bitter-sweet, but it was Edinburgh's vicious climate that sent him abroad in search of better health. He died in Samoan exile in 1894 from a brain haemorrhage.

to my parents! . . . O Lord, what a pleasant thing it is to have just damned the happiness of (probably) the only two people who care a damn about you in the world.'

Of course, it was never the same again at home. But Stevenson's essential reasonableness, his caring, his kindliness, his concern for others, as well as his independence, vitality, his determination and courage to stick to his own beliefs, doubly hard for someone so gentle, so cursed by ill health, were also the qualities of the writer. Unconsciously perhaps, but the writer in him was taking over, storing away such events, the heated emotions, the stilted dialogues, the anguished hurt and emptiness. Who knows if David Balfour's quarrel with Allan Breck, his dearest friend, on the bleakness of Rannoch Moor was not part re-enactment of that tense scene in 17 Heriot Row? The same loss of logic, the same bitter words to be regretted, the same sense of unreality, the false poses, although in *Kidnapped* it all had a happier ending.

But Stevenson did become the great writer. The sheer simplicity and readability and sincerity and compulsion of his writing, often at lightning speed, the projection of those secret thoughts and emotions of childhood in his poems, the reflection of himself in everything that he wrote, created an audience of readers by the million worldwide. The tragedy of R.L.S. was that he had the spirit and vivacity and energy and the will to fulfil so many other adventurous ambitions, but it was all locked inside that fragile frame. He arose feeling ill and went to bed feeling worse. For years on end. How he was able to write at all at times is remarkable. So much of his life was spent writing from a sick bed or travelling the world, often in poverty, in search of the health he never found.

That red-bearded extrovert William Henley, who lived in Thistle Street and was part-model for the character of Long John Silver, disliked by Fanny Stevenson, once adored by R.L.S., wrote one of the best descriptions of Edinburgh's favourite writer, who died in Samoan exile in 1894 after a brain haemorrhage:

> Thin-legged! thin-chested! slight unspeakably,
> Neat-footed and weak-fingered; in his face —
> Lean, large-boned, curved of beak, and touched with race,
> Bold-lipped, rich-tinted, mutable as the sea,
> The brown eyes radiant with vivacity —
> There shines a brilliant and romantic grace,
> A spirit intense and rare, with trace on trace
> Of passion, impudence and energy,
> Valiant in velvet, light in ragged luck
> Most vain, most generous, sternly critical,
> Buffoon and poet, lover and sensualist;

A deal of Ariel, just a streak of Puck,
Much of Anthony, of Hamlet most of all,
And something of the Shorter Catechist.

R.L.S. was the last of the New Town's own writers to be recognised on the
world stage. The New Town connection with Hugh MacDiarmid is tenuous,
although half a century after Stevenson, as Christopher Murray Grieve, he was a
student teacher at the old Broughton Higher Grade School in Macdonald Road,
before going on to become a major influence on Scottish verse. But the New Town
has been host to many literary 'memorials of their times': Arthur Conan Doyle, who
lived in Howe Street, and took Edinburgh surgeon Joseph Bell as his model for
super sleuth Sherlock Holmes; Lewis Spence, in Howard Place, influential poet
and, like MacDiarmid, a founder of the Scottish National Party; Bruce Marshall,
who took pot shots at R.L.S.'s sitting duck target of Edinburgh's middle class in
the 1920s; actress and novelist Rebecca West; historian George Scott-Moncrief;
Orcadian Eric Linklater with Magnus Merriman; Muriel Spark with Jean Brodie;
the intellectual poet and writer Edwin Muir; that agreeable font of all knowledge
New Town, writer Moray MacLaren; that jolly, understanding, able poet and
delightful man of feeling Sydney Goodsir Smith, whose verse leads this chapter;
his friend and co-writer in Scots Robert Garioch Sutherland; fellow Royal High
School boy and schoolmaster Norman MacCaig; the colourful Sir Compton
Mackenzie who latterly gave animated audience in Drummond Place from a
reclining position in bed or clad in a 'heavy-weight champion's' day-glow dressing
gown; Albert Mackie, the poetic journalist, who reported run-of-play soccer
matches in verse and as McNib poked fun and burst a few ego bubbles with his
sharp-witted four-liners; J. K. Annand, another schoolmaster poet with a deep
understanding of children, who delighted their parents as well with his
Bairnrhymes in Scots for the old *Weekly Scotsman*; Alan Bold with his top-o'-the
Walk beginnings . . . there are countless poets, writers, editors and publishers
(without whose risks and sound judgement many celebrities would still be
hopeful unknowns), who have stepped on the New Town stage or had a jar or two
or five in the Abbotsford or Daddy Milne's or the Cafe Royal or The Doric tavern
of Jimmy McGuffie's day.

Of course, the parade of celebrities and characters who have played out their
part against the backcloth of the New Town across two centuries tends to adopt a
retrospective vividness that makes their counterparts of today appear muted. Or
have their numbers diminished? Or as financial houses and office blocks replace
homes and people, is corporate image and identity now more important than the
individual? Certainly many senior executives of leading companies in the city,

who at one time automatically would have been public figures, keep their heads below the parapet in low profile. It is a double pity because not only does Edinburgh need all the free-ranging characters it can muster to retain its traditions, but under those corporate hats are personalities and talents who have much to offer Edinburgh, but too many are only superficially involved in its affairs.

In the early colourful years those 'Modern Athenians' of their day came from the ranks of judges and advocates, politicians, churchmen, bankers, businessmen, academics, publishers, artists and writers. A goodly gathering of Scots judges, more than a dozen at the last count, active and retired, have continued to make the New Town their home, although it is hardly possible, or even seemly, for a judge nowadays to express personal opinion without being chased by the media if he breaks cover from the corporate image of the judiciary. To qualify as a Modern Athenian in the 1990s it is not necessary, however, to return home down the Mound on a skateboard as some of those uninhibited judges of the old order might have attempted (although not so long ago wig-clutching legal figures were seen leaping on a chalked peever bed in Parliament Square). What is a Modern Athenian? There is no definition. Except that they are 'different', and it is not enough merely to be a prominent figure. But Edinburgh folk have been reared with them for centuries and recognise the breed immediately.

In the New Town today the two Lord Camerons are unquestionably Modern Athenians. Father and son, patricians, The Edinburgh Academy background, the same passionate interest in the New Town's antiquity and its wellbeing. Lord 'Jock' Cameron, now with a long and distinguished legal career behind him, a conversationalist of urbane delight, a yachtsman and painter of the seascapes around the shores of Loch Broom, a great supporter of the New Town who has done much to serve its interests as President of the Cockburn Association. And Loch Broom himself, Lord 'Kenny' Cameron, a judge who really looks like one, tall, elegant, but with a twinkle in the eye and a fund of amusing anecdotes in the right company, the former Lord Advocate, the sharp end of the Scottish legal system.

Another legal family eminently qualified are the Emslie 'bookends', as the Heriot Row neighbours call them. Lord George Emslie, retired Lord President of

OPPOSITE

Sir Compton Mackenzie — in the best tradition of a New Town character, this colourful writer and personality made his home at 31 Drummond Place. A founder member of the Scottish National Party and deeply committed to the Scottish cause, it was comic novels like *Whisky Galore* that brought him popularity, although critics admired him in more serious mood.

the Court of Session, at one end of the most sought-after street address in the city, and his advocate son at the other. Regarded as one of the most enlightened members of the bench in recent times, it was always viewed as a scoop when Lord Emslie accepted an invitation to dinner. But rather than be on the negative end of an Emslie judgement on their evening, meticulous hosts would often prompt guests with an advance memorandum to the effect that 'golf is a proper subject to discuss with his lordship'. And it always was, time and again, even for dedicated non-golfers. After years of distinguished service at the summit of the Scottish bar, Lord Emslie must have retired with one of the finest collections of golf stories in the country.

Round the corner lives his successor, Lord Hope, and the very act of being both Lord President and a New Town resident means instant acknowledgement as champion of the principles of Scottish justice and guardian of New Town traditions. Lord Clyde, also in Heriot Row, takes a keen antiquarian interest in the New Town, like his father before him, and his grandfather before that, all former pupils of The Edinburgh Academy, and in the case of the Lord Clydes, duxes no less. Back in 1946 James L. Clyde, King's Counsel, had already been singled out as a Modern Athenian by artist Tom Curr with words by the late Lord Provost, Sir Will Y. Darling, a most notable Modern Athenian himself, and published in book form with other Athenian contemporaries. Sir Will's verse went:

> King's Counsel he — and much beside,
> Law the garment with Politics the hems.
> Will Tweed at Peebles, choosing Clyde,
> Send him to speak — for us — by River Thames?

In fact, he did not win this particular seat for the Conservatives, but instead he went on to become the member for Edinburgh North and later one of Scotland's most senior judges.

Still in Heriot Row, in its most famous house, No 17, is the Dunpark residence with height-of-season tour buses halting outside every few minutes to explain that this is where Robert Louis Stevenson once lived and, no, it is not open to tour parties. As a judge, Lord Dunpark was capable of raising an eyebrow into the hairline from time to time with his High Court sentencing, but he was always his own man in the best tradition of those old days' judges, a student of human nature, a pioneer of the informal chat with children, and his understanding and humanity in dealing with family cases stand as a proud tribute. The discretion of judges does not apply to wives, thank goodness, and Lady Dunpark has never been known for her silences. Fondly remembered by many as the Tory 'toun cooncillor' Kathy Macfie, who at times appeared to have as much in common with Labour councillors as with those in her own party, she makes up for all the public inhibitions of all the judges put together. She is the genuine, direct link with those splendid and delightful characters who graced the New Town a couple of centuries ago and, like them, refreshingly speaks her mind, but in an Irish country brogue that has withstood even the filing influence of New Town society (she was once sent to a fine English boarding school to tone the accent down but instead the other girls developed Irish accents). She should use it more often nowadays to speak out on Edinburgh's behalf. Apart from her city of adoption, Lady Dunpark's passion is for R.L.S., and perhaps because of the Irish blood as well as the red hair, she cares and feels the spirit of R.L.S. more than most. Certainly No 17 has never been in safer hands.

And what about the brothers Daiches, most worthy Modern Athenians of the purest order all their lives? Lionel, Q.C., also of Heriot Row, his name linked with courtroom dramas and famous trials, most elegant raconteur, sharp of mind and riposte, such agreeably good company, a storyteller of delicious protraction, who could have taken his place on the bench but chose to be a great defence lawyer instead, so often accepting legal aid cases, as you would expect. Professor David, living at the western end of the New Town, brilliant academic, cultural historian, biographer of Burns, Boswell, Scott and Stevenson, expert on English literature, but first love Scotland and, because of his knowledge of Scotch whisky, the man you would most wish to choose your dram. The sons of Dr Silas Daiches, the much-respected former Edinburgh rabbi, together they make a celebrated and distinguished New Town family, most assuredly Edinburgh memorials of their time.

Lt. Col L. P. G. 'Leslie' Dow, late of the Cameronians and veteran of many Edinburgh Military Tattoo spectaculars as its producer, is an extrovert soldier of character and engaging good fun, which is fitting because in the early days the New Town was well populated by the military. He should have been christened LMG Dow for the rat-a-tat orders that emitted from the producer's box high above the stand, unheard by the audience, but things don't always go right on the night in a live show, and his commands were jumped to in best military fashion. He is one of the leading 'Monks of St Giles', that marvellous old Edinburgh society which continues vigorously, where crazy dinner nights are punctuated every few minutes by charity forfeits and members and guests literally sing or recite for their banquet supper, while the 'monks', in their brown habits, collect the 'fines'.

Perhaps Oliver Barratt, the indefatigable secretary of the Cockburn Association, should have been a soldier with his talent for drawing a bead, then letting fly and hitting those who threaten the New Town's architecture or

Lord Clyde — as he appeared to artist Tom Curr in 1946 as James L. Clyde, King's Counsel. But there are two other distinguished Lord Clydes — his father and his son, the present Lord Clyde, all duxes of The Edinburgh Academy and later judges. The family home is in Heriot Row.

amenity. Or a professional journalist or all-in wrestler or a politician. When a New Town predator is encountered, there is no one more creative in the art of graphic description or the selection of bludgeoning or scalpel words or the grappler's range of armlocks or the matching rhetoric. Most of the time, however, these talents are hidden away behind olde worlde charm, easy and engaging, and the sheer knowledge of his subject. Oliver Barratt's name may bring groans from those who deal in easy options, but given his pursuit of what is right for Edinburgh — and who but the Cockburn Association is the most reliable judge on that score? — then the louder the groans, the greater the reassurance.

Guilleasbuig Macmillan, Minister of St Giles', Dean of the Thistle, Chaplain in Ordinary to Her Majesty the Queen, lives in the New Town although his charge is uphill on the Royal Mile. A preacher from the intellect as much as the heart, a supporter of the establishment but disengaged from it, a counter-puncher in words, but you must listen hard for the humour in the cleverness, and those who know him well speak of his warmth, wit and caring. His is the independent opinion, often the unexpected, the challenging, and with all these attributes he could step back in time and climb easily into the pulpit of old days' Edinburgh and feel at home. With a Christian name like Guilleasbuig (it means bishop's servant) it is no surprise that time-distant Mull and Appin, Oban and points Argyll declare themselves as his voice gathers sermon momentum. They are personal performances all, the best he can give, not just for a congregation that treks up from the New Town, or drives in from Corstorphine, Barnton and Morningside to hear his word, but also for those visitors who enter Scotland's great High Kirk for the first time, merely passing through, but still expecting a virtuoso performance from the minister. The job has its recompense. In a city where the official luncheon or dinner is ritualistic, the pronouncer of grace is in demand, which at least guarantees that the New Town's minister of St Giles' eats rather well.

As a West Coaster with his heart in the Highlands, Professor Sir Robert Grieve has settled for the New Town's more peaceful life in retirement after a career as mountaineer, chief planning officer for Scotland, the chair of Town and Regional Planning at Glasgow University, the chairmanship of the Highlands and Islands Development Board and many other adventures. The spirit and resolve that made them successes are disguised by the studious manner, the quiet voice, the considered comment, the total absence of pretension. Bob Grieve is the New Town's philosopher, his perspective on Scotland seen through the eyes of the poet influenced by a lifetime of balancing social and economic disciplines. His priorities are clear: the simple things are the important things, dawn on the Mamores, the beauty of the changing Edinburgh seasons, the distillation of thought through verse, the search for knowledge, the caring about people, causes and environment. It could be the philosophy for Scotland, and it is heard over lunch in the Arts Club.

In his redoubt at the foot of the Mound, below the Grecian columns of Playfair's National Gallery of Scotland, surrounded by shades of his favourite colour, dull red, in the leather upholstery of his chairs, reflecting wine red from the walls, that imported Modern Athenian from Birmingham, Timothy Clifford, Director of all the Scottish National Galleries, surveys the art world restlessly. 'They call me "Tiger Tim",' he says with a smile, meaning presumably the Edinburgh art establishment, which has not quite recovered from the Clifford whirlwind which hit the city half-a-dozen years ago. Tim Clifford moves fast, talks fast (pity the shorthand writers), thinks on his feet, and expects to see his thoughts realised in glory before he sits down. He is also formidably knowledgeable about his subject and dedicated to furthering the interests of his various charges, one way or another. It is a style and policy that can be abrasive, volatile and self-projecting, but it also achieves results, and apart from running onto Princes Street and stuffing fine art into the eyes of the masses, he has achieved the next best thing by persuading an additional quarter of a million of them through his stately portals each year to view talking-point masterpieces in his refurbished gallery. Ideas and plans burst from him, his suits are like zebra crossings, he is the controversial maverick in the Scottish art scene but with the virtue of having the good humour and sense of fun to also see himself as others see him. He mirrors many of those singular or unconventional characters who peopled the early New Town.

The names of New Town leading leeries come thick and fast. Former chairmen of Scotland's two great banks have made their homes in the New Town, Sir Thomas Risk, of the Bank of Scotland, Sir Michael Herries, once a Hong Kong Taipan, of the Royal Bank of Scotland, highly respected public figures both, maintaining the image and reality that it is men of calibre, integrity and of international ranking who head Scotland's financial institutions, contributing much of themselves to personally further the New Town's interests. Angus Grossart, the merchant banker of Queen Street, another respected figure, quietly plays a part in supporting Scottish arts. James Gulliver, central figure in the battle for the Distillers company, is now a New Towner, diverting some of his energy into handsomely sponsoring the performing arts. Alastair Darling, Loretto background, an advocate, the credentials for a Whig or Tory a couple of centuries ago but now, with his distinctive piebald look of whitening hair and darkling beard, the esteemed Labour member for Edinburgh Central, cares deeply and actively about the future of the New Town, his home. Menzies Campbell, the Scottish Liberal Democrat member for North East Fife, advocate, supporter of the Scottish cause, former sprinter of renown at both the Commonwealth and Olympic Games, captain of the United Kingdom athletic team and a record holder, now has his eye on political glory from his home in the New Town, which he loves. Lester Borley is Director of the National Trust for Scotland with Charlotte Square's Georgian House the apple of his eye. Magnus Linklater, editor of *The Scotsman,* practises his journalistic skills from North Bridge which gave the New Town life, in the city so well known to his writer-father. Dr Selby Wright, wartime BBC padre with a congregation of ten million and former minister of the ancient Canongate Church; author Joan Lingard; artist Sir William McTaggart; Sir Lewis Robertson, the business doctor who improves the health of companies; doyen photographer Broderick Haldane: there are so many names, so many personalities, characters, financiers, surgeons, architects, academics, civil servants, town councillors, some in the news today, some household names of yesterday, some rising stars ready to take their place, a seemingly self-perpetuating community of notables, going about their business, strolling the streets like their counterparts across those centuries, doing their shopping like ordinary mortals, plastic shopping bags at the trail, stuffing groceries into gold-initialled briefcases in their favourite Pakistani's or their mince and sausages from Willis's in George Street. If you know where to look, they are part of the city sights, Modern Athenians in their natural Georgian habitat.

Bid them good morning. They are a reassuring sight. Their numbers may be reduced, but there are still plenty of them. They are a sign that not too much is wrong with Scotland's capital and there is plenty of life in the old New Town yet.

CHAPTER FIVE

NEW TOWN STROLL

'CITY OF EVERYWHERE, broken necklace in the
        sun,
you are caves of guilt, you are pinnacles of
        jubilation.
Your music is a filigree of drumming.
You frown into the advent of heavenly hosts.
Your iron finger shatters sad suns —
they multiply in scatters, they swarm
on fizzing roofs. When the sea
breathes gray over you, you become
one lurking-place, one shifting of nowheres —
in it are warpipes and genteel pianos
and the sawing voices of lawyers. Your
        buildings
are broken memories, your streets
lost hopes — but you shrug off time, you set
        your face
against all that is not you.'

Norman MacCaig

'NOW I want you to look at Edinburgh,' the guide is saying. 'I mean really, really, really look at Scotland's capital. And listen. I mean really, really listen — and you will hear the centuries speak.'

She stands on the top step with her back to West Register House, the old St George's Church in Charlotte Square, dwarfed by its giant columns. Pens hover above notepads to record her pearls of historical New Town data, eight cameras are slung forward for fast flashing action as her entourage commence their walking tour of Georgian Edinburgh.

'Pliz spik more loud. Too big traffics noises,' requests one of her charges. And the centuries also go unheard.

'Lord Cockburn, the famous judge and social commentator, lived over there at No 14,' the guide continues with undaunted enthusiasm. 'And Sir William Fettes, founder of Fettes College, was his next door neighbour at No 13. Note Robert Adam's "palace front" architectural masterpiece on the northside, a central colonnaded unit, adorned with carving, flanked by plainer houses. See how the end wings protrude and are decorated with flat pilasters. Earl Haig, one of the First World War's most famous generals, was born in No 24. Professor Lister, celebrated for his pioneering work in antiseptic surgery, lived in No 9 from 1870 to 1877. At one time Charlotte Square was known as Edinburgh's Harley Street because of the number of doctors and surgeons who resided here. Now it's almost all big financial companies. Some call it the richest square in Scotland. Over there in the gardens is the fine equestrian statue of Prince Albert, consort to Queen Victoria, who unveiled it in 1836 . . .'

She is stopped short in mid spout.

'Get picture of Prinz Alberts, pliz.'

The group manoeuvre the Charlotte Square racetrack with a hop, step and final leap to reach the oasis of tranquillity at its heart. Through iron railings and locked gate they peer at Prince Albert obscurely from afar, too distant to photograph or even admire. Where, asks one, is the way in?

'There's nae wey in, Jimmy,' comments a helpful native. 'Ye've had it. Ye'll meybe breck the gress.'

A shimmy to avoid an open-topped city tour bus, oops! almost a stumble, and they gain sanctuary in the National Trust for Scotland's Georgian House at No 7, as Lester Borley, the Trust's director steps smartly out, smiles a welcome, murmurs a pleasant good morning in accent southern and strides off towards George Street, while housekeeper June Turnbull ensures all is pristine for a new day. And the rules state no photographs will be taken there either.

On the southside a white-thatched skyscraper called David Birrell, Edinburgh knowledgeable about city affairs and legal figure of character, enters Dundas & Wilson, Writers to the Signet, where he has served a lifetime, as colleague Robin Edwards, CBE, pops out to confirm a property deal and Euan MacLeod dashes to court; Sir Charles Fraser, of W. J. Burness, one of Scotland's leading lawyers, and Ivor Guild, of Shepherd & Wedderburn, leave almost simultaneously by car from their respective offices for different destinations; Willie Munro, chairman of the Scottish Building Society and Edinburgh dynamo for Tenovus-Scotland, has strolled over from his Manor Place headquarters and momentarily engages a friend in discussion near the Roxburghe Hotel, owned by Edinburgh tycoon David Murray, chairman of Glasgow Rangers and, look, there's manager Walter

Smith and players Mo Johnston and Trevor Steven popping in for a pre-match foregathering; big Hamish Coghill, assistant editor of the *Evening News* and local historian has peched up from Oxford Terrace to head for North Bridge; Graeme Manson and John Colquhoun airt down Glenfinlas Street together to their office of RMD, chartered accountants, symbolised by a chess set knight on their brass plate in Great Stuart Street; heads turn as an imposing limousine with the intriguing number XXI swings down towards Hill Street and Heart of Midlothian chairman Wallace Mercer quick marches out to don his other hat as chief executive of Dunedin Property Investment Co Ltd.

It is a moment frozen in time. A snatched photograph in a 1990s' Charlotte Square time warp. People passing randomly. The centuries meaningless. The stage remains. The New Town continues. Seconds later it could be a different snapshot, another time warp, chance meanderings and meetings or secret assignations, and someone says, hey, there's the Secretary of State going into Bute House, or the Moderator leaving his official residence, or Betty Kirkpatrick, lexicographer, on her way to the Arts Club, or Patrick Bourne, the art dealer, with an Anne Redpath under each arm, or publishing consultant Paul Harris in a jacket that dazzles, or Lady Lucinda Mackay out to purchase oils for a new portrait, or fellow artist Jemima Blackburn or Mardi Barrie or Sheriff Ian McPhail or Lay Constable Tom McGlashan passing almost unnoticed on the other side of the square. Or an earlier decade or century or two and it is Dr Andrew Thomson, leaving his St George's pulpit or surgeon James Syme in No 9, or Lord Neaves at No 7, Lord Robertson at No 42 taking a constitutional, Lord Chief Commissioner Adam, one of Sir Walter Scott's friends, at No 31, or Sir John Sinclair of Ulbster in No 6 waiting for his carriage. They are New Town spectres, time travellers on that fascinating stage. Or it could have been Lord Cockburn enjoying the country hush at evening, with the green fields and woodlands beyond. Or today Lord John McCluskey, wig set aside for the weekend, strolling from his house in the west of the New Town, or Lord Grieve or Judge David Edward, of the Court of First Instance of the European Court of Justice, in Luxembourg, feeling good to be visiting home again.

Along George Street not a car space is to be found and the wardens free range. That butcher of quality, T. G. Willis, at No 135, with its reputation for charitable generosity and exotic haggis, declares neutrality in the daily outfoxings between drivers and wardens with a window card stating 'No change given for parking meters'. Smiling faces appear from Aitken & Niven's, youngsters clutching new rugby boots, hockey sticks, a larger school blazer, scarves of Heriot's, Watson's, St Margaret's, St George's, Stewart's-Melville and The Edinburgh Academy to the fore. Pensive faces emerge from the Solicitors' Property Centre, a billion pounds' worth of houses for sale, packaged in vertical displays by area and price: intakes of breath, knowing looks exchanged, clasps of hands to brows in mock horror. But ask yourself, dear, are two bedrooms in Moray Place really worth £120,000? But, darling, think of the address. Pocketing their free pencils, they continue the discussion outside.

Visitors are taking coffee in the St John's Church Centre, creating havoc with the banana cake, or are upstairs in Willis's or taking luncheon quiche in A & Ns or afternoon tea in the Edinburgh Book Shop, sipping, munching, gazing idly, butterfly blethers, staring out of the window — 'Just look at those four little iron balconies across the road, aren't they sweet, Elmer, up high, do you see them, they must be from olden times.' Indeed they are, and look at the balustrades and window ornamentation on that unpretentious Bank of Scotland next door, worth cashing a cheque at No 64 just for a peek at the ceiling. And look around. Bits of 'olden times' are everywhere, displayed the length of George Street. Look closer. Behold! A permanent exhibition of classical architecture — Greek, Italian, Gothic influences, Georgian, Victorian Establishment, Victorian Baroque, buildings that are ornate, bold, stern, overbearing, retreating, amusing, delicate, confident, strident, exquisite. Observe them in detail. The fine classical carvings and figures along the Standard Life, the noble columns of the TSB, the stately portals of the Royal Bank of Scotland with its five reassuring pillars crowned by a splendid relief, the sculptured stone above the National Westminster's impressive bronze columns, and look at Gray's at No 89 — some ironmongers! — squashed refinement with its Coat of Arms for supplying cleaning materials to the Royal Family. Textured stone, sculptures, balconies, friezes, flagpoles, classical overtones, hardly a building that is not a character.

Now there is a tiny, flashing lighthouse above the door at No 84 and inside sit the Commissioners of Northern Lighthouses, with the Lord Advocate and Solicitor General for Scotland heading the team, its beginnings back in 1786, with Robert Louis Stevenson's family playing a major role. Now automation is the objective and even the Isle of May Lighthouse in the Forth is remotely monitored from George Street. But the old romantic names, legends — and dangers — continue: the Bell Rock, the Abbot of Aberbrothock, Sir Ralph the Rover, Skerryvore and the other Skerries, Muckle Flugga, Tod Head, Buchan Ness, Hyskeir, and all those other lonely, storm-lashed, life-saving outposts are administered from below that little flashing light at No 84, where Commander John Mackay, MBE, holds command. And look, just round the corner, a small plaster bust of Sir Walter Scott above the door of No 39 North Castle Street, where the great man penned some of his best-known works, his house now occupied by Messrs Murray, Beith and Murray, Writers to the Signet, but now no one quite seems to know where his beloved study was located, and the chances are it is giving inspiration to the typing pool.

ABOVE AND OPPOSITE

Elegant homes, elegant dining rooms, the early wealthy New Towners knew how to look after themselves. Dinner parties were important social events and some bordered on the exotic. Enormous quantities of food were consumed and washed down by equally vast amounts of drink. All the main meals, including breakfast, proffered many choices and solon goose, buttered crabs, oysters and pigeon could be on the menu simultaneously. Sophisticated dinner parties in fine surroundings are still part of the New Town scene, particularly among the senior legal profession and business community. Our pictures show a fitted kitchen and dining room of the period 1807-1815 taken in the National Trust for Scotland's Georgian House at 7 Charlotte Square.

Ah, but there is someone really well known in George Street who knows everyone worth knowing. Why, it's Joe Pullar, ex-Royal Scot, at his newspaper stance at the intersection with Frederick Street. One of the old school, 40 years

in the business and his father before him, about 80 years between them on that draughty corner, Joe a newspaperman to his blue fingers and frozen toes, at the sharp end, who understands his patch and with a story or two to tell about the changing New Town. Aye, it's for the worse. 'Hello, Joe, terrible weather, *News* please.' 'Here ye are, darlin', nice tae see ye.' 'Hello, Joe, *The Scotsman,* thank you.' 'There ye are, m'Lord, ah think ye're in it the day, how are ye keepin'?'

And look, it's the Rev. Andrew McLellan, minister of St Andrew's and St George's, calling in to see how the organisation for the May book sale is progressing, all proceeds to Christian Aid, his church a Sunday pleasure, gone the soor-dook faces of sabbaths past, of hoodie crow Sunday braws, funeral suits and hats, the bitter dissension days of the Disruption, now a welcoming handshake on the pavement as the bells toll at 10.50 a.m., shining faces, laughter, children, kilts, sports jackets and floral dresses, warm welcomings, kissings of greeting as the organ belts it out from within, but with Lindsay Sinclair at the keys, more accurately described as a virtuoso performance. And there's Councillor David

Disappearing Edinburgh . . . David Rhind's magnificent Life Association of Scotland building on Princes Street with David Bryce's New Club on the left were both demolished in 1963. Above: the light-coloured modern edifice in the centre of the picture is what replaced them and it may be the shape of things to come on Princes Street. Some may prefer the new look, but Princes Street could ill afford the loss of such heritage as well as the dignity. Behind its modern façade the new New Club carries on in old worlde elegance and style as always. In the foreground is the most photographed house in Edinburgh — the delightful and colourful cottage in Princes Street Gardens.

Guest, checking out car numbers reported for unauthorised parking in Gloucester Lane; and Harry Bremner, of Vogue, parking his Mercedes in front of the George Hotel where he once parked his battered carpet van; and there's Robert Sowersby, manager of Cunningham's, the surviving hat makers in Scotland, one of the oldest shops in Edinburgh, founded in the reign of George III, now down by the bus station, but some of the finest people in the country visit him to have their Cunninghams fitted.

And look at Princes Street, see how those flashback iron balconies and railings also remain a theme from earlier years, now fragmented, isolated virtues. Note the row of curtainless top-floor windows, almost its full length, signifying space unutilised. Look at Jenners — the outside, that is — the ornamentation, the fine sculpturing, the miniature columns, the flagpoles, the dignity. Even the Old Waverley Hotel next door states its architectural preference for Edinburgh's older days, like Romanes & Paterson and the Edinburgh Woollen Mill, occupying buildings clinging perilously to another age, shouting 'this is the real Edinburgh', but muted against the dominant modern design next door in the clone character of other cities throughout the world.

And look at that other modern wonder between Nos 80 and 86 (expressing the character of 21st-century Princes Street?), and think of Bryce's architectural gem that once stood there and is now lost to the city. And look, there's Lord James Douglas Hamilton about to enter by an unassuming doorway, but graciously he pauses to allow Professor Alan Thomson and Alastair Dunnett to step out into the throng unremarked, but first a gentlemanly acknowledgement. Here is the New Club, arguably the most exclusive club in Britain, haunt of the famous, the notable, leaders in many fields, public faces, some elder statesmen with their power bases long behind them, others at the core of Edinburgh and Scottish decision-making today, senior politicians, academics, judges, financiers, surgeons, businessmen, advocates, distinguished civil servants, soldiers of rank and bankers of influence. Behind that unlikely modern exterior and untrumpeted entrance, the old order reigns triumphant, little changed in atmosphere or even furnishing from last century, a sense of collective mateyness, the friendships of familiarity, fine paintings, *objets d'art*, agreeable lounges with full-frontal dramas of Edinburgh Castle in floor-to-ceiling windows, a discerning bar surrounded by wit and laughter (but not too loud), luncheon orders personally scribbled in advance, tables spaced for privacy under the watchful eye of Queen Victoria.

Across the road Tom Barkley, parks officer in Princes Street Gardens, exits left two youths who thought flower beds were for running across, an elderly couple take out their flask and sandwiches, nod approval and settle down to listen to the music from the Ross Theatre; a young man with three days' growth to his chin and crumpled coat to his back snores peacefully at full stretch on a bench marked 'Presented by members of the Berlin Philharmonic'. Look at the benches! Hundreds of them, arm-to-arm in ranks, presentations all, sweet memories, sincere gestures. Stroll over to the West End, the organ playing Mendelssohn in Palmerston Place Church, and the Rev. John Chalmers joins the wedding party on the steps for a photograph, while three little girls watch the bride with dreamy-eyed rapture; passing some of the most attractive basement gardens anywhere — astonishing what can be done with a few tubs and imagination — and some disgraces, all company-owned; in Hanover Street a procession of emergencies are admitted to the Doll's Hospital; David Ingram, antique dealer of repute and look-a-like for the Laughing Cavalier, watches the break-up of the big, old New Town houses with regret from his shop in North West Circus Place and, as chairman of Stockbridge traders, wonders how long it will be before changing cost structures mean small local businesses like butchers, bakers and grocers will have to be subsidised — and he's only partly joking. In Stafford Street another character with flowing locks to his shoulders, Charlie Miller, man-about-town and world-traveller in the hairdressing business, finds his diary booked for the next two weeks, a personal accolade for the stylist — in more ways than one — who began snipping in Bob's in the West Port at 2s 6d a skull when Perry Como's and the Tony Curtis were almost obligatory; in Wavereley Station British Rail's area manager, John Dingwall, dusts down his ceremonial bowler, for a royal personage is arriving; Councillor Mo Rizvi checks out more parking complaints; in Dean Park Crescent the St Bernard's Education Centre still has 'Infants' and 'Juveniles' carved in stone above the entrances from its old school days, and a burglar alarm is the symbol of modern times; round the corner in Danube Street not a car space is to be found, which would not have pleased Nora Noyce, Edinburgh's most famous madam, who once ran her brothel here in Georgian elegance; down in Henderson Row and along the northern fringes the New Town is being reconstructed, but small children from the new flats are playing there again; and community life is thriving with the restoration of old blocks like Clarence Street, built in 1831, reborn 1987, courtesy of Edinburgh New Town Conservation; and there's 73-year-old Mrs Blank, widow for nine years, living alone up a Georgian stair and pondering the proposed split of conservation costs with her eight neighbours and deciding not to become involved because 'ma hoose will see me oot', so she goes shopping instead along the fancy St Stephen Street, now the browsers' paradise, from Agnes Croan's flowers to Mr Purves' lighting museum. Through the gateway of what was once Stockbridge Market an elderly couple examine with fascination the old iron clothes poles in the little garden; and on an eavesdropping stroll along Hamilton Place, outside the store Mrs McCruncher — which is not her real name — regales two cronies with the riveting conversation stopper, 'Is it no' awfy that some folk cannae keep their mooths aff their neebours, that Mrs McWhustle, she's at it again, oh hud yer tongue, here she comes!' And as her friends move across the road to Stockbridge Primary, Mrs McCruncher's greeting follows: 'Hello, Mrs McWhustle, ah wis jist talkin' aboot ye, how's yer man's sair back . . . ?'

Towards the 8.30 a.m. bell-time skeins of children are still making for Broughton High School, singly, in groups, a fashion parade of T-shirts and anoraks, the female of the species more vivid than the male, trailing back in multi-coloured strings uphill to the New Town, idling, chattering, munching, monkeying, yawning, pushing, chasing, but always converging on Carrington Road. There is a perceptible quickening of pace around 'in' time, a few pell-mell last-minute sprinters, a tearful girl eight minutes late, a few Joe Cools conserving energy and reputation in slothful procession: the later they are, the slower the footrate. The last of the stragglers is a full 20 minutes after the rest, no rush, a leisured kicking of an empty coke can, an apple in one hand, a cigarette in the other, the last few yards to the sidegate a bite and puff synchronised with every step, until with a flick of both wrists core and doup simultaneously make perfect parabolas onto the pavement and another school day is confronted.

Inside work is in full swing, computer keyboards clattering, screen cursors pulsing, the language laboratories interrogating in French and German, the science rooms analysing experiments, the sound of excellence drifting from the music unit where those specially-gifted children from all over Scotland polish their talents, players shouting their lines from the school theatre, while the tantalising aroma of browning sausage rolls wafts from home economics as a big modern school with a distinguished record and some 800 pupils aboard gets on with the work. Sniffing around. 'Where's the library?' 'I'll take you, sir.' Helpful boy. Browsing, delving into present achievements, Broughton antecedents, the McDonald Road era, old photographs, magazines, the school record assiduously kept: summer term 1915 has been singularly uneventful, the monotony only broken by visits of H.M. Inspectors — how we welcome these important personages in our midst! That's interesting — 'C. M. Grieve is now known as a poet', George Ogilvy, head of English at the time, rejoicing in the words at the early recognition of his friend. And here is a school magazine for Christmas 1939 and headmaster T. P. Black is saying, 'We are the poorer for the loss of many of our pupils and several of our staff . . . you cannot in such times fully control our destinies by foresight and prudence, but you can, and must, have faith in whatever new conditions of life may emerge; vigour in body, culture of mind and integrity of character will prevail'. And look at this! A poem by Hugh MacDiarmid, that same C. M. Grieve, former Broughton teacher, now poet of international standing, writing 'To those of my old school who fell in the Second World War':

> So, to-day, hope lies
> In the free and many-sided spirit of humanity
> Against one-man Domination.
> Beyond the meaningless and dead splendours of Versailles,
> The glowing beauty of Chartres
> Speaks imperishably through the ages.
> And even so will the future see you,
> Little groups of comrades of my old School,
> Who went out
> Against the Powers and Principalities of Darkness.

OPPOSITE
One of the pleasures of a stroll through the New Town is looking at its basements. Many have become garden delights and works of art. Unlike some cities there is no social reproach in living below street level and a number of Edinburgh public figures are happy to descend to their little heavens and rear gardens. The picture shows the attraction of Northumberland Street enhanced by a combination of stone, iron, potted plants and hanging baskets.

ABOVE AND OPPOSITE

The Stockbridge area has always been considered something of an artists' quarter and the successful conservation scheme in little St Stephen Street reflects that impression with the development of a string of informal speciality shops of character. Appropriately opposite the former Stockbridge Market it is a higglety-pigglety collection of antique shops, an astrology centre, a gramophone emporium, a school of dancing and drama, shops that sell glass, clocks, clothes, pots, flowers, books and the useless sundry oddments that someone somewhere always wants. It spreads into the basements and there are also some pleasant pubs and eateries. The pictures show Mr Purves's lighting museum and the corner turning into St Stephen Place.

Hail and farewell, my friends!
At the moment it seems
As though the pressure of a loving hand had gone,
The touch
Under which my close-pressed fingers seemed to thrill
And the skin divide up into little zones
Of heat and cold whose position continually changed
So that the whole of my mind, held in that clasp,
Was in a state of eternal movement.
My eyes — that were full of pride,
My hands — that were full of love,
Are empty again — for a while,
For a little while!

Across the road Fettes College rears in towered and turreted magnificence, grand, exclusive, elite, dominating the surrounds for miles, but for the pupils of Broughton High School it might as well be in Hong Kong or Disneyland. No communication, no involvement, not even a sporting challenge. Except some Broughton pupils use its manicured lawns as an unofficial shortcut. They have little enough in common: Broughton is local, day, state and free; Fettes attracts pupils internationally, it is private, 85% boarding, and fathers measure the years in thinning locks and school fees to be paid. But their objectives are almost identical: both are dedicated educationists, both strive to foster individual talents, to achieve academic qualification, to foster self-confidence and independence, to take their places responsibly in society. But in their own way. The juxtaposition of the two orders 100 yards apart with such similar ambitions, so much to offer each other but with such massive disinterest is remarkable. Yet there is common ground: just inside Fettes main entrance Birnie Rhind has created in stone a sculptured masterpiece to the Fettesians who died in the First World War — just as Hugh MacDiarmid created the same sentiments in verse for his fallen Broughtonians. And high on a window on that extraordinary Fettes facade of architectural genius some school wag has hung a notice proclaiming 'No poll tax here'.

OPPOSITE
'For we are very lucky with a lamp before our door', wrote Robert Louis Stevenson and though Leerie, the gas lighter, does not make his rounds these days No 17 Heriot Row, R.L.S.'s New Town home, still has its light and the verse is appropriately engraved upon it. His bedroom was on the first floor front and it was from these windows that Cummy, the outspoken Alison Cunningham, held the sickly little boy in her arms to gaze out on the passing scene below.

On the other side of Fettes Avenue, The Edinburgh Academy Geits (primary 7) third team are playing school rugby at New Field. Fifteen small boys line up in their blue-hooped jerseys. The roar of the crowd is in their ears, David Soul in their hearts, their country beckons. Eight dads, three mums, several younger brothers and Rover are on the touchline to lend vocal support and pick up shattered dreams if necessary. The day is a soaker, conditions a mud bath. Tiny legs tire fast, kicks are measured in centimetres. Minutes to go and it's odds-on for a no-scoring draw. Then suddenly The Academy break away, a neat passing movement demanding appreciation even from Jake Young, and the home team scores a try. A diminutive figure steps up to take the kick. It is long and difficult and on the gluepot surface he has as much chance of lifting the ball above knee-level or even reaching the posts as he has of jumping the bar from a standing position wearing concrete boots. But he doesn't see it that way: he envisages a clean kick with the power of a rocket dead centre between the sticks to land somewhere in Fife. And so does the captain of the other side, an even smaller figure, tears of despair held back bravely at the prospect of defeat, the full burden of responsibility dropping on his halfpint shoulders as he takes up a strategic position within earshot of the kicker. A deep breath, a pause before commencing the run-up to glory, and the opposition captain's voice rings out in explosive emotion — 'Miss it, you bastard, miss it!'.

Up by Heriot Row that indefatigable band of New Town visitors still listen to their guide with close attention. She stands before Robert Louis Stevenson's house at No 17, an arm raised pointing: 'It was behind that first-floor window that the sickly little boy had his bedroom. His nurse Alison Cunningham would wrap him in a blanket, hold him close in her arms and they would look out onto the street together. This is where the lamplighter came. Yes, just where we're standing. And over there in Queen Street Gardens is where the young Robert Louis Stevenson played. The bushes and glades and trees were like an adventure land for him. He had a wonderful imagination. There is a little pond in there that is said to have given him the idea for *Treasure Island . . .*'

She is stopped short as she prepares to move on to new fascinations.

'Get picture of pond, pliz.'

'Sorry', says the guide. 'These are private gardens. The gates are locked. Only residents have keys.'

CHAPTER SIX

CHANGES

'AULD REEKIE through the keeking glass
Looks fine, and sae it does.
And the mornin and the evenin
Were anither age gain by.'

Sydney Goodsir Smith

WHEN the first brick of the New Town's first house was laid in Rose Court in 1767, Robert Burns was a boy of nine, Horatio Nelson was eight, Napoleon had yet to be born, George III was king, America was becoming an increasingly irksome colony, and Scotland's capital had a fast-rising population of 60,000. Dancing assemblies were the rage, the men favoured three-cornered hats, dressed wigs, knee-britches, fancy waistcoats and sported swords at their sides. The ladies arrived by brightly-painted sedan chairs, a link-boy in front to light the way and chaperoned by a valet. They wore wide-hooped skirts, powdered wigs, embroidered petticoats, and if there was a crush on popular dance nights they were requested to remove their hoops to make more space on the floor. The dancers faced each other from opposite ends of the hall and the twain never met unless by permission. Outside an area was designated for waiting sedans, like car parking today, and promptly at 11 the ladies were whisked home.

The oyster bars were the places for higher kicks. Ladies and gentlemen sat together around long, rough-hewn tables to devour large quantities of best Forth oysters 'as fat as e'e can gaze on'. They were served on huge dishes with a plentiful supply of porter to wash them down. They talked a lot, laughed a lot, danced reels, and as the evening developed and the punch and brandy flowed, the stories became increasingly rich, the laughter more shrill and some of the attractive young fishwives could even be persuaded to dance on the tables. It was all great fun, the fashionable thing to do, and a hard night at the oysters attracted the best people in town.

Food and drink were important to the better-off families, partly because they enjoyed them, but also because it demonstrated knowledge of a subject associated with gentility and sophistication. Good food knowingly prepared in overflowing abundance, presented with discernment and fine wines was a display of wealth as impressive as flaunted jewellery and the imaginative quality of the dining-room table became a talking point and way of life for many New Towners. They took breakfast around 10 a.m. in those early days and it was substantial: both hot and cold meat was served in quantity, fish and fowl, rolls, scones, coffee, cream and marmalade. Dinner (what we call lunch today) was served in the Old Town about 2 p.m., but across in the New Town, considering the time it took to walk or take a carriage home from business, it was delayed until 4 or 5 p.m. It was another banquet: venison, mutton, beef, veal, pigeon, eggs in gravy, buttered partans (crabs), rabbit, solon goose in season from the Bass Rock and fried flounders could be the dinner offering. It was an age of heavy drinking and no meal was complete without porter, punch and good French wine and the diners were more likely to give up before the supply gave out. Of course, no work was contemplated after dinner, but supper had yet to come and this again amounted to a feast: a typical late evening menu might read finnan haddies, eggs, bacon, devilled kidneys, curried rabbit, oysters, baked partans, partan pies and minced collops. The ancient statistics tell their story, and in the year ending 1776 around 9,000 oxen were consumed and 41,000 sheep. It is little wonder that colic was one of the major ailments of the day. As time passed, dinner and supper began to merge. Such were the demands and quickening lifestyle of modern 19th-century Edinburgh that the breakfast call was even advanced to 9 a.m. The rat race had begun.

Today's pressures have introduced the American-style business working breakfast at 7 a.m., Broughton High School pupils begin lessons at 8.30, for some office workers lunch is a tuna-and-sweetcorn sandwich from Martins, prawn-and-cucumber from Crawfords or British Home Stores, eaten on the hoof or at the desk or gulped in Princes Street Gardens or the warmer climes of the St James Centre on a green bench or a pie-and-pint or fast-food pub-grub from a multitude of New Town establishments. And for a select few, company and political decision-makers mostly — and those they woo, inform, confide in or indulge — a more leisurely 1 till 3 expense-account, high-living luncheon in the George Hotel or Raffaelli's or the Balmoral, with little business contemplated thereafter, but just like the old days, dinner is still to follow. Food and alcohol remain a passion today for all walks of life and age groups and there are more outlets than ever before to serve their desires. Even nightshift workers can enjoy their pint at dawn — a far cry indeed from when 'Time gentlemen, please' sharply shut city oases just as the evening was beginning to warm up and in Edinburgh's time perspective that was only yesterday.

The poor were still dying of starvation as the New Town was built. And from the complaints and conditions that accompany poverty. And from the alcohol intake to try to forget it. Tuberculosis was the dreaded killer, but cholera, typhus and smallpox were recurring epidemics and little could be done until their lifestyle and living conditions were changed. They made the best of what could be procured cheaply. Boiled sheep's head was therefore always welcome in the house, so long as the wool was well singed, tripe and onions were tasty and nutritious, trotters could be presented in a number of ways, herring were inexpensive and even served to prisoners in the old Calton Jail, a pot of powsowdie (sheepsheid soup) could last days, and Scotch broth with everything intilt was a mainstay. Potatoes and porridge at any time were acceptable, but when the price of wheat rose, many families were forced to change to white bread with a spoonful of jam or treacle and cup of tea as a main course, the forerunner of the jeely piece, but it was of substantially lower food value.

Beer was always popular, and William Younger's brewery in the Holyrood Sanctuary had a drouthy clientèle. Younger's Edinburgh ale was a potent fluid, wrote Robert Chambers, which almost glued the lips of the drinker together and of which few could dispatch more than a bottle. In 1778 there were 2,011 licensed houses in Edinburgh, around eight licensed stills and 400 unlicensed; by the beginning of the 19th century a drinking outlet of sorts was on hand for every 130 inhabitants, purveying a fascinating range of firewaters, devilish brews, and wines, but whisky still held pride of place. The popularity of claret, which tended to be drunk in private houses, began to wane towards the end of the 18th century. When the duty on claret was raised in 1780, playwright John Home was moved to verse on the outrage:

> Firm and erect the Caledonian stood,
> Old was his mutton, and his claret good,
> 'Let him drink port', the English statesman cried —
> He drank the poison and the spirit died.

In the New Town in the 1990s weekend binges remain a problem as 'outsiders' flock to the centre of town. Wine enjoys new popularity, late and early licensing has caused controversy as the hardline Victorian influences on the purveying of the demon are relaxed along Continental lines. The spit-and-sawdust drinking dens of the past have gone, the community pub is almost a community centre, the wonders of plastic have revolutionised pub design, although thankfully the New Town retains some traditional gems reeking with last century character. The humble fish supper, first-choice diet of generations of the not-so-well-off, is still king, but now no longer cheap and with many rivals; a dip into the deep freeze produces an array of fast-food TV snacks and the new baked potato shops offer a tasty morsel directly linked with those bad old days, but now with exotic dressings.

And an extraordinary occurrence that would have caused incredulity and derision if such a suggestion had been put to 19th-century Edinburgh imbibers — alcohol-free drinks are carving out a profitable slice of the beverage market.

Poverty has not disappeared. Even in the centre of the New Town, yards from the richest square in Scotland, it is present in several guises and ranges of depression. The down-at-heel but familiar figures who at one time paraded New Town streets were recognised as being poor because their appearance declared it. They have mostly all gone along with the professional scranners who plagued bucket day. Now the signs of poverty are more subtle, better camouflaged, less obvious but equally distressing. The elderly dignified widow living below the breadline in historic splendour with her pride for company and little else is a well-known New Town phenomenon. The large student population struggles to make ends meet, as George Street bank managers confirm, because parents are not always supportive and creative financial geometry still cannot project inadequate grants to meet necessary outlay no matter how thinly they are extended. Young marrieds who have misjudged the property market and its costs, jobless youngsters caught in the benefits trap, down-on-their-lucks who share a bench, a building site, a shelter . . . they are all present, their distress as acute as in any other community, except that the sculpted stone and wealth of New Town financial houses act as a foil to their misery.

It is to the credit of many New Towners of all walks of life that they rally round and keep a watchful eye on older members of their community. Good neighbourliness is not the prerogative of working-class areas alone, and acts of great kindness, generosity and compassion do take place in the New Town as in any other community, some of them by caring public figures who would wince in embarrassment if their private good deeds were known. And as in all communities, there are also those who are so entirely untouched by poverty themselves that somehow they cannot conceive of its existence.

In an ancient city like Edinburgh the changes that take place over the centuries stem from the consequences of what has gone before. The human condition forces change, pain and aspiration mostly, and the will to improve. Looking back through Edinburgh's centuries, the causes and effects of history, the links with the people of the past and the people of today are obvious.

In the New Town of 1850, Princes Street was cobbled, iron lamp-posts with their hissing gas mantles stood every 30 yards, and the tall chimney of the gas company rose high above street level from its position below North Bridge; many of the original private house railings were still in place on the pavements, canvas awnings fluttered outside the shops and big, plodding cart horses delivered their goods; hansom cabs were the taxis of the day and they were in abundance like the street dung, which was collected in piles by hand carts. Not for nothing are the roses in Princes Street Gardens in such vigorous health. Even then it was a busy scene, women doing their shopping in ground-sweeping dresses, shoulders covered by capes or cloaks, parasols to the fore, not a bare head in sight. The preoccupation with hats was still at its height, menfolk displaying the most creative variety, and even children had their caps or bonnets in place, but not always socks or shoes for their feet. A massive wrought-iron gas candelabrum of light, sprouting a flowering head of five globes, stood in the middle of the road at the intersection with Waverley Bridge and urchins enjoyed sitting on its stone steps to watch the world pass by at horse pace.

In 1850 First Class rail passengers from Waverley Station were offered travelling peace of mind by paying 3d to insure their lives for £1000 every time they stepped on a train, and if their fancy turned to more distant journeys, a payment of £10 would buy them steerage passage, full provisions and 20 acres in Natal under the government's emigration scheme, with Willie Bowie of 17 South St David's Street delighted to make the arrangements, the threat of Zulus, Boers and apartheid still in the unseen future; a Friday to Monday excursion to London cost 42 shillings or you could sail from Leith to Hull for 7 shillings.

In 1850 in the New Town whisky was 12 shillings a gallon, Lochfyne herring 4 shillings a keg, finest stubble-cured Dutch butter was 10d a pound, American cheese 6d and French macaroni 10s 6d for a 16lb box; a dress coat was 16 shillings, tweed trousers 7s 6d and James Graham, the hosier, was offering the very latest in undershirts — the celebrated 'Zephyr' no less — for four bob; a John Wightman piano from his shop at 23 St James Square was £20.

In 1850 the property market was buoyant and 21 Moray Place went on the market at a roup sale in Cay and Black's premises at 81 George Street at an upset price of £2,900 with a feu duty of £31 3s 6d; and James McPherson, a Leith plumber from Constitution Street, was making a small fortune from New Town householders by installing the latest in self-acting water closets as part of his modern sanitary improvements, which introduced the new-fangled effluvia traps. Michael Wilshire, from his gutta percha shop in St David's Street, suggested that if you were going down to Portobello sands for the day he would render your shoes impervious to salt water, elegantly, economically, immovably, endurably and firmly.

In 1850 health quacks were tempting the gullible with a multitude of pills and potions for almost every ailment. Ford's Pectoral Balsam of Horehound claimed astonishing healing effects on the 'emaciated and those wasting away from consumption of long continuance'; Roper's Royal Bath Plasters, Powel's Balsam of Aniseed, Dr Locock's Pulmonic Wafers and 'try-ere-you-despair' Holloway's Pills were all aimed at relieving chronic chest disorders, shortness of breath, coughs and dropsy. Parr's Life Pills guaranteed 'good health, good spirits and long life' at a shilling a box; Lady Hesketh's Pills had 'remarkable effects' on cases of indigestion, habitual costiveness, irregularity of the bowels as well as removing flatulence. New Towners flocked to Scott & Orr, the druggists, at 78 Princes Street to buy them.

In 1850 teeth were not neglected, but if they were beyond repair dental surgeon James Dobie, of 7 George Street, undertook to supply artificial teeth that would 'restore articulation as well as mastication and return the mouth to its original utility and beauty'. Rowland's Odonto or Dentifrice imparted 'a pearl-like whiteness' to teeth, and during the Christmas period when 'friends and lovers assemble at the social board and are put under more than usual anxiety to create PERSONAL ATTRACTION the following unrivalled discoveries for the TOILET are called into increased requisition, namely — Rowland's Macassar Oil for creating and sustaining a luxurious head of hair and Rowland's Kalydor for rendering the skin soft, fair and blooming'.

In 1850 New Towners were dedicated to self-improvement, and little private schools were active throughout central Edinburgh: Mr Oliphant's School operated from 33 Charlotte Square, MacDonald's School concentrated on English at 56 George Street, M. Guillerez had a French Academy at 27 Castle Street. Shops and businesses long forgotten were thriving where the big multiples draw the customers by the thousand today. Dr Mein was a popular New Town dentist at 94 George Street, Mr J. Boyd gave careful and minute phrenological examinations of the head at No 45, Richard Whytocks sold fine carpets at his shop at No 9, J. & W. Fairley had the largest stocks of umbrellas and parasols at 27 Hanover Street, Eagle & Henderson were leading nurserymen at 81 George Street, Caldwell, the stationer, of 15 Waterloo Place, boasted a substitute writing implement for the goosequill, a three-pointed pen — 'invaluable for swift writers' — and James Durham, of 7 George Street, produced the writing material to go with it.

In 1850 pleasures were simple but Edinburgh entertainment was even then setting international standards. A vocal and orchestral concert in George Street's Music Hall played to packed houses with Madam Sontag rendering melodies from Russia, Siberia, France, Hungary and Croatia at 7 shillings for centre seats and 2 shillings for the back gallery. In the evening there was a switch of style and pace as M. Jullian presented a new Grand Quadrille and two new waltzes and polkas and you could watch for a shilling from the gallery. At the Theatre Royal *A Comedy of Errors* proved popular, Professor Anderson's grand and wonderful entertainment of natural magic was a winner at the Waterloo Rooms along with The Grand Conundrum Night, which required three exclamation marks on the publicity bills to do justice to this great contest of wit for the magnificent Silver

Cup (value 20 guineas); in the Hopetoun Rooms Madam Montenegro, the Prima Donna of Her Majesty's Theatre, London, with Signora Santiago and Senor Mantelli, restored the international flavour in a full dress operatic concert, while in Queen Street Hall Mr and Misses Fraser held musical and literary evenings with a highpoint rendering of 'A Cottar's Saturday Night' as 'brought out by them in London and in the principal towns in England with great success'.

Progress! Half a century is the blink of an eye in Edinburgh and 50 years later, on January 1 in the year 1900, the wonder of cinematography had arrived and the talk was of war. Twenty-five thousand Boers had gathered at Ladysmith, it was reported, and the British generals were expected to attack their positions beyond the Tugela at any moment. The Modern Marvel Company's camera team had just returned from the dark continent to present 'British Army Embarcation Scenes, Colonials on the March, the Maxim Gun in Action, the Latest Transvaal Incidents to Hand, Heroes of the War etc., the Best, Prettiest and Closest Animated Pictures of our Gallant Navy and Army'. They may have been in flickering shades of black and white, soundless, disjointed, breaking down frequently, but they were newsreels of a major world event in which our land and sea forces — no air force then — were again in action and therefore they made gripping and compulsive watching.

On the same bill the cinematograph revelation displayed its versatility by jointly presenting the 'grand Christmas pantomime of Cinderella, realistic and truly wonderful, quite sensational and beautiful, in fact', and tickets were available at 3s, 2s and a shilling, children half price, from Paterson & Sons of 97 George Street. *San Toy*, a Chinese musical, was more traditionally playing the Royal Lyceum, *Babes in the Wood* at the Empire, *Dick Whittington* at the Theatre Royal and H. E. Moss's 'very grandest, most varied, original triumph of a Christmas and New Year carnival' was spellbinding the multitudes of Edinburgh citizenry every morning and evening in the Waverley Market. A Miss Clara Butt, vocalist, later a London superstar of her age, made her first appearance at the Music Hall, where Madam Clara Samuel attracted the crowds for her Grand Scottish Concert with a rendering of 'Willie's gaen tae Melville Castle', nobly supported by the choir singing 'Scotland Yet'.

The January sales of 1900 also drew the crowds. Henry Darling of 124 Princes Street offered Paris model dresses and dinner gowns at half price. Furrier John Bently, of 29 Hanover Street, innocent of the controversy his trade would attract in decades to come, offered fur necklets from 12s 6d and fur muffs up to 12 guineas. In a seasonal message of goodwill published in *The Scotsman*, Robert Maule & Sons, of the West End Emporium, announced that their first thought on that first fresh morning of a new century was to wish everyone a Happy New

Year. 'May increased happiness be found in every home in this first year of grace', wrote Mr Maule, 'the garners of all kept full from the horn of plenty, and may our nation be blessed with an early dawn of peace.'

In 1900 the Edinburgh Hydra Hotel boasted tramcars to the city centre every 13 minutes, a male secretary from a New Town business could command a salary of £30 a year, a cook £28, a 'strong, early-rising' kitchenmaid £14 a year. As the new century opened, No 45 Heriot Row was up for sale by public roup in Lyon & Turnbull's George Street rooms at an upset price of £3750 for three floors, attic flats, three front cellars under the pavement and a back green; and a first-floor flat at No 8 Eyre Crescent was quoted at £450.

In 1900 policemen wore helmets, ladies bustles and fancy hats, the flat 'bunnet' was increasingly in evidence for working men, lace and celluloid collars were the 'in' fashion for small children and they could be purchased at the johnny-a'-thing shop at No 8 St Stephen Street, which also purveyed potted head, tobacco and cigarettes, Sunlight soap, fireworks, groceries, hooks and eyes, wine and spirits, confectionery, balloons, pins, firewood and briquettes, and even low-cost wash-day mangling took place in the back premises. George Street was gloriously free from traffic, not a television aerial or dish or parking meter was to be seen anywhere.

Today the first £1,000,000 town house in Heriot Row is in sight, yet the same turn-of-the-century pantomimes continue their magical Christmas tradition — Aladdin still calls up his genie, Jack climbs his beanstalk, the babes are still being lost in the wood, and although new hero Jamie makes an occasional Edinburgh entrance in search of his wish, it is less likely to be realised now because there are substantially fewer live shows and theatres as well as cinemas. Television has done for the lot. Even Jacey's news theatre and later the Monseigneur News Cafe at 131 Princes Street, which offered well into the Sixties the 'world's best entertainment' of news, cartoons, travel and a cuddle in the back row, could not compete with the wee box in the corner.

Today slashed-price January sales are still as popular as ever and woo bargain hunters by the mob just as they did in 1850. But fashion-conscious Victorians would now look askance at the New Town street throng. Dressing up to go shopping on Princes Street was habitual until recent times, and although some of the most elegantly dressed people in Scotland still parade central Edinburgh in head-turning vignettes of pavement haute couture and sartorial splendour, the Casual Nineties look reinforces the trend for jeans, sweaters and trainers, and today they predominate among the less formal younger generations. The Victorian verdict on Princes Street today would be that much dignity has been lost over the years, along with some of its architectural gems and once-famous quality stores like Darlings and R. W. Forsyth, reflections of a calmer age of shopping serenity.

Bustles, pavement-sweeping dresses, fancy hats and parasols are the height of fashion in Princes Street in 1898. It was an age of hat-wearers and even the children sport a variety of head attire. The photograph was taken near the top of Waverley steps and a rank of horse-drawn carriages await fares just like the taxis of today. Sandwich boards were a popular means of advertising and the bowler-hatted parader proclaims that McLaren's of Princes Street is the best diner in town.

Jenners, of course, continues to lend tone to Princes Street as it has done since the young Charles Jenner opened for business with his partner Charles Kennington in 1838 when their rented property at the intersection with St David Street cost a mere £150 per annum. The two young men had been fired by W. R. Spence, the Waterloo Place drapers, for taking a day off work to go to Musselburgh

The sun is out on Princes Street and so are the crowds. It remains one of Europe's premier thoroughfares, but in comparison with older days its quality fades and the popularity of this "half a street", with shops on one side only, owes much to its striking position looking over the valley to the Castle and the faerie skyline of the Old Town. The Nelson Monument and a corner of Edinburgh's designer ruined Greek temple rise above the throng.

races, but by then they were convinced they had the experience they needed to go it alone. Quality, style and pride have been the Jenners' ideals ever since. It is a policy that has made them an Edinburgh institution. They have survived wars, recessions and a disastrous fire, they have served royalty and many of Scotland's leading families, no task has been too trivial to be carried out with dedication, even to sending a reel of cotton to a regular customer in the Borders by that special Jenners' delivery van or at one time employing three commissionaires to ensure an open-door welcome. They have raced additional supplies of handmade chocolates to the royal box at the King's Theatre to catch the interval, donned steel helmets to firewatch from their rooftop vantage point in case of German raiders while dispensing glengarries and regimental ties to the military below. They have witnessed worthy competitors unable to withstand today's ferocious commercial pressures close their doors for the last time on Princes Street. Somehow Jenners have managed to adapt, to read the changes in advance and move with the times. Sometimes they have had to make harsh decisions, rethink policies and services, broaden their appeal, attract more customers, but they have done so without lowering standards, perhaps even improving them, and it has been achieved by efficiency and the pleasantry of their staff with their attention to detail. The influence of the Kennedy family from as early as 1857, when the young James joined the company as a lad of 13 from Thornhill in Dumfriesshire, has been critical to Jenners' success and the dynasty continues into its fourth generation with Robert Douglas Miller at the helm. They have made Jenners one of the most remarkable quality stores in Britain and they remain the royalty of Princes Street. But such is the speed of change and the cut-and-thrust of modern commerce that today the Burger King and its band of lesser starlets also make bids to rule and change the face of what is still one of the most attractive shopping thoroughfares in Europe.

The two great hotels at either end of Princes Street have also set style and tone and architectural significance for almost a century. They were built at the time of the great railway boom when competition between rival companies for passengers even led to looking after their creature comforts and some of the finest hotels in Britain came into being at that time. The striking Balmoral, until recently the North British Hotel and known to most of Edinburgh as the 'N.B.', towers above Waverley Station looking as if it has been newly erected after its recent refurbishment. It was the apple of the North British Railway Company's eye. At its west-end terminus the Caledonian Railway Company built its rose-coloured Princes Street Station Hotel, later the Caledonian Hotel but more affectionately known locally as the 'Caley', and such was its opulence that it boasted passengers who stayed there would be treated 'with almost royal magnificence'. Its telegraphic address was 'Luxury, Edinburgh'. It too has recently been given a facelift. The two competitors opened within a year of each other, the North British throwing its doors open first in 1902 with a glittering launch party. The old 'N.B.' took seven years to build and cost £225,000. Today's restored Balmoral cost £20 million pounds. In those early days when a large double room cost around 8s 6d and a coal fire an additional 1s 6d, the two hotels were in deadly competition and the managements glowered at each other across Princes

LONDON AND FRENCH WAREHOUSE,

47, 48 & 49, Princes Street.   2, 4, 6, 8, 10, 12, 14 & 16, S⁰ St. David St.

EDINBURGH

B. Purvis Russell Montgomery Esqʳ

Hattonburn.
Milnathort.

Bo⁼ of **Charles Jenner & Company,**

Silk Mercers, Linen Drapers & Haberdashers.

READY MONEY.
Prices marked in Plain Figures.

14/95

1910								
Sepʳ	2	3	Shirts	5/6		16	6
		3	Vests	4/6		13	6
		1	Hat			2	6
	15	1	Vest			7	11
		1	Pants			8	6
	30	2	Pyjama Suits	10/9	1	1	6
					£ 3	10	5

+

Aug.	13.	½ dozen Collars	8/6		4	3
				£3	14	8

RECEIVED PAYMENT
WITH THANKS,
5 OCT. 1910
CHARLES JENNER & Co

Street Gardens. As the years slipped by, however, respect grew and even friendship, and for a time they had the same owner. Both hotels have welcomed royalty, prime ministers, heads of state, film stars and the famous from all over the world. Even Trigger, the Wonder Horse, has been led up the Caledonian Hotel's grand staircase by his pard, the singing cowboy Roy Rogers and wife Dale Evans back in 1954, a distinction shared with Mario Lanza, Paul Robeson, Mary Pickford, Gene Kelly and Laurel and Hardy. It was proclaimed at the time Trigger spent a sumptuous night in one of the hotel's best rooms, specially equipped for the occasion. But as one little Edinburgh boy commented the following morning, gently clutching a lump of Trigger's dung in his cupped hand and with eyes shining in proud ownership, 'It wisnae true'. Like other mortal horses, Trigger slept in a nearby stable.

One of the main concerns in the New Town today is increased crime, with drugs a new misery, and central Edinburgh is a weekend target. The booze is in and the wit is out on Friday and Saturday nights, as has been a pattern longer than anyone can remember, once associated with pay and having a rest day. Now there seems to be an undercurrent of violence and viciousness that was not present at the beginning of the century. The number of serious assaults in a four-square-mile area around the New Town makes disturbing reading, yet a perspective is to be drawn: considering what happens in other cities and the fact that some six million tourists visit Edinburgh annually and seldom encounter even a cross word, never mind a clenched fist or swung boot, Edinburgh remains one of the world's safer cities. The shoplifters move in at the weekend, too, some of them visitors included in the tourist statistics, and present Princes Street with its biggest policing problem. Hordes of them work singly and in teams, light fingers crossing the socio-economic boundaries, the irony being that in today's better-off society the problem should multiply. But the shops have never been so stuffed with pinchable goods, so invitingly packaged, and in the Nineties the morality of right of ownership apparently is stood on its head. Or is it all about the excitement of the challenge these days of not being caught? Or is today's society having an extended flirt with lawlessness? And would being 'brint on the cheek with yin

OPPOSITE

It is 1910 and a shirt cost 5s 6d. The bill is made payable to Charles Jenner & Co, silk mercers, linen drapers and haberdashers of 47, 48 and 49 Princes Street and 2, 4, 6, 8, 10, 12, 14 and 16 South St David's Street, exactly the same shop and site of Jenners today. The prices may have increased, but the Jenner's tradition of quality still continues. As the bill was being written the clip-clop and rumble of horse-drawn vehicles outside would be punctuated by the rattle-and-roar of an SMT open-topped charabanc — the motorised traffic jam was on its way.

key', as happened to thieves in the old days, make society more law abiding? That is an argument we have heard somewhere before!

There has always been thieving in Edinburgh, but today we are spared the gangs of women slinking over from the Old Town at gloaming, enticing New Town children into darkened alleyways, where they were stripped of every stitch of clothing, left howling, naked and freezing before the female marauders slipped back to their 'fence' somewhere on the High Street. And in recent times there has been nothing like the public outrage over the infant murders by Stockbridge baby farmer Jessie Kean in the late 1880s. How many adopted babies 'disappeared' was never established, but the emotions of New Town women in particular were so stirred that some even volunteered to act as her executioner.

Probably the worst case of murder the New Town has experienced took place even before it was built. Mr James Gordon, an Edinburgh businessman from Aberdeenshire, had his home on the hill down towards the village of Broughton in 1717. The tutor to his two young sons and daughter was Robert Irvine. He took a liberty with a servant girl and the young boys innocently informed their father. Gordon properly reprimanded Irvine, who lapsed into a brooding sulk, plotting revenge. The following Sunday Irvine took the Gordon boys for a walk among the gorse and grassy braes that are now St Andrew Square and York Place, where they chased butterflies and gathered wild flowers. Suddenly Irvine's sense of injustice boiled over. He accused the little boys of being tell-tales. He screamed that they must be punished. The *Domestic Annals* of the time recount how the boys tried to run away, but Irvine easily overtook and seized them. 'Then keeping one down upon the grass with his knee, he cut the other's throat, after which he dispatched in like manner the remaining one.' The whole gruesome scene had an eyewitness, and after trial, which took place the following day, Irvine was sentenced to death by the Baron-baillie. He had his hands struck off before being hanged at Greenside and the hands were then fixed to the gibbet by the knife used upon the boys. This grim slice of local history clarifies the meaning of being caught 'red-handed' and illustrates the kind of swift summary justice that was dispensed, and that the processes of law ground somewhat faster than today!

The passage of time brings many changes, and one of the most disconcerting is that the Englishing of the New Town is nowadays accelerating. Simply fewer Scots voices are heard among residents and fewer Scots words are being used. The Englishing influence has been present almost from the beginning, of course, and Edinburgh with its trappings of government, its concentration of national institutions, major companies, an important university and famous teaching hospital has brought an ebb and flow of many nationalities which has always been a welcome feature of Capital life. Many of them have chosen to make their home in the New Town. But with the soaring of the property market a New Town house or flat is suddenly an exceedingly attractive investment, and the extraordinary property boom in the south, a bubble which appears now to have sensibly burst, has enabled Home County property-owners in particular to sell up and buy grandly north of the Border. Desirable Georgian Edinburgh with its elegant lifestyle, quality infrastructure, historical background and star-shooting house values has been an obvious magnet.

Over the last five years the general pattern has been for central Edinburgh houses to reach remarkable prices, and those with the necessary ready capital have tended to have English rather than Scots tongues. This may or may not be to the advantage of the New Town in the long term, but it remains a fact and it can be interpreted that Scots at this time are being priced out of it. A little England in the heart of Scotland is emerging and, like little tartan Scotlands in odd corners of the world, many of our southern cousins seem quickly to have learned how to assume Scottish identity and espouse Scottish causes. And good for them! Apart from their Englishness and accents they integrate well. Some have important jobs at senior executive level, some are even in charge of our national institutions. Perhaps in a setting like the New Town such a trend has little significance. It has no discernible power base or political aspiration and is no more than the same speeded-up process that has carried on for two centuries. But if it continues at the present pace and the trend is projected forward a few more decades, then the Englishing of central Edinburgh will be substantial. As it stands, it is not without influence. Even at the most basic level fewer Scots accents are heard, fewer Scots words and phrases are used and the erosion of the Scottish vocabulary in the Scottish capital, indeed in the very part of the city which was the haunt of Burns, Scott, Stevenson, MacDiarmid, Goodsir Smith, Norman McCaig, Albert Mackie, Robert Garioch and the others who felt that the Scots language was important enough to write in it, is that much less likely to be halted. And as the words go, the culture is threatened, and when you lift your eyes to view the perspective of all the pressures on Scottish culture these days throughout the whole of Scotland, suddenly a few discontinued words become precious. Otherwise who is going to read Fergusson or Burns or MacDiarmid or the other Scottish versifiers for pleasure and meaning? And who hopefully will then be their successors?

It would be entirely wrong to lay all the problems surrounding the Scottish language at the door of incomers, of course, and Scots words have been disappearing too fast for too long. Words that were in commonplace use by Edinburgh grandfathers, less so by their offspring, are hardly heard nowadays. Sadly, in spite of an academic interest in Scots language in a national context, Scotland's capital is hardly even associated today with either preserving Edinburgh words at street level or creating new ones. Glasgow appears to have taken the lead in this respect and a healthy trend in Edinburgh's great rival city is to give the problem the Glesca nod, so to speak, 'pittin' the heid oan it' to replace old words and phrases with new ones, new patter, which, in Glasgow parlance, is pure dead brilliant.

A dreich Saturday morning at Goldenacre and Heriot's rugby-playing schoolboys troop off the field droukit and covered in glaur. Today the weather is unpleasant and they are covered in mud. Yet 'glaur' has a sense of constituency and 'a glaupen o' glaur' translates badly as a handful of mud. But when did you last hear 'glaur' used?

'Pit the telly aff, he gies me the scunner', and Terry Wogan would be none the wiser anyway. 'Scunner' is now almost exclusively the vocabulary of the over-fifties in Edinburgh, but was there ever term more tellingly descriptive?

'Haud yer wheesht, ye'll wauk the bairn an' Mrs McClumpher fae next door'll stert her girnin'.' 'Wheesht', 'girn', words overladen with meaning and expression, but they are under a death sentence.

Think of those old Scots proverbs and sayings. The wit was in the thought, but the effect was essentially of language:

Edinbury haar will weet an Englishmen tae his skin.
Better a finger aff than aye waggin'.
It's an ill cause that the lawyer thinks shame o' it.
Ye're nae chicken for a' yer cheepin'.

Gurly. Wersh. Trauchle. Lowp. Canty. Clart. Smeddum. Unco. Speir. Begowkit. Shilpit. Grue. Dirl. Pech. Bourach. Braw. Forfochten. Caller. Coldrife. Mirk. Thrawn. Chiel. Glaikit. Reek. Airt. Ayont. Havers. Fleg. Stramash. Aiblens. Feckless. Couthie . . . there is a whole dictionary of them: a rich, colourful language that is languishing for want of use. And vanishing.

'A'hl gie ye twa steelies for a muckle jaurie an play ye for yon bonnie glessie' was once the lunchtime conversation in the old Broughton School playground as the boys played bools or, to avoid confusion, marbles. In the old New Town, outside the fashionable parts, to the north side, the east and west, and down in Stockeree, the streets were the places where tradition was kept alive by the young generations. 'Aleavo!' or 'Releavo!' were the shouts from under the street lights as a sprinter detached herself from the shadows to enter the 'den' and release her team-mates caught by the 'het' gang. They would scatter in all directions with shouts of 'Ye canny catch me fur a wee bawbee!'

The girls' peever beds chalked on the pavements tended to be mysteries to the boys who thought them cissy, but they were quite happy to join in stookies or have cuddy fights or play kick-the-can or fitba' with two bricks or jaikets for the goalposts. Going back even further, those streets once echoed to the trundling sound as the iron girds went into action, and if yours had a cleek or cleet, it was the top of the range. There is many a New Town grandad who took part in a gird race in Broughton Street or along Henderson Row, dodging the prams full of washing on their way to the steamie, or around Hamilton Place or Stinkie Lane or throughout the lower end of the whole of Georgian Edinburgh who could still show a touch of class wrist-action at a sharp corner. Peeries or tops were also once the passion and it took skill to keep it spinning with the help of a whip. 'Awa' an' whup yer peerie' was a parting insult as friends fell out. 'Awa' an' whup yer ain' would come back the rejoinder.

For years it was the girls who kept links with the old order alive with their skipping and stotty ball games in school playgrounds and along the pavements. Skipping still continues and the rhymes move with the times, but the bouncy ba' against the wa' is disappearing fast if not altogether. Some of their chants echo over the years off the New Town's Georgian walls:

> Early in the mornin'
> Afore eight o'clock
> You should hear the postie
> Knock, knock, knock.
> Up laups Teeny
> Runnin' tae the door
> Wi' a one a letter
> Two a letter
> Three a letter four.

> Miss Broun went tae toun
> Wi' her knickers hinging doon.

> The big ship sails roon' the eely ally-o
> The eely ally-o, the eely-ally-o,
> The big ship sails roon' the eely ally-o,
> On the last day o' September.

They had circle games, elimination games and the games that only small children understand. They were innocent and happy, and those who remember can grieve a little, for many have gone forever along with lost innocence:

> As ah wis goin' doon the street,
> Ah saw a scabby donkey
> Ah one it, you two it
> Ah three it, you four it
> Ah five it, you six it,
> Ah seven it, you ATE it.

Eenty teenty number nine
Dip yer neb in turpentine
Turpentine will mak' it shine
Eenty teenty number nine.

Oor wee Jeannie
Wi' the nice clean peeny
Guess what colour it was?
Rid. R-e-d spells Rid
And rid you must hae on. You are oot.

Eenty teenty fingerty fell
Ell dell demon ell
Urky purky tarry rope
An tan toosie Jock.

They were the days when kirk pews were full, when the fishwives with their creels and traditional costumes came up from Newhaven and took their chance around New Town doors with brush salesmen, rag-and-bone men, knife and scissor sharpeners, Brittany 'ingin' johnnies with their bicycles of threaded onions, buckie wives with their cockles and mussels, when 'Gramophone Granny' Russell played her wind-up gramophone outside the old Playhouse Cinema, when George Paterson, the 'Frederick Street Fiddler', entertained shoppers just up from Princes Street, when John Cadona was a star street attraction as a one-man band and when Mrs Dunlop with her hurdy-gurdy barrel organ, pulled by Smokey the little white pony, particularly around the Melville Street area, was a great fascination for the children. Both Mrs Dunlop and John Cadona played the streets of Edinburgh into the Sixties and they were the last of a long line of entertainers. Now with by-laws relaxed, the buskers are the street turns and some promising talents are revealed, especially when some of the music students come down from the University to practise their pieces and earn a bob or two at the same time. The big lad with the Mohican haircut and the punk outfit who occasionally performs outside the Royal Scottish Academy has the makings of a piper. But are they as good as Swing Charlie, the blind musician, Albert Parkin with his fiddle and wee dog, Poemy Dick and his melodeon, or the singers Davie Arkley and Jamie Mair when they used to descend from the Old Town to do an occasional turn in the longer ago?

Princes Street was a focus for the trams and they were a great fascination for children. Firstly the horse-drawn jingled its open-topped way between Bernard Street in Leith and the Haymarket on November 16, 1871, with bells fitted to the horses' harness to warn pedestrians of its advance, and the driver had a whistle to

Poet Allan Ramsay stands on his stone pedestal above the Floral Clock at the foot of the Mound and surveys the passing scene. The shape of cars, the trams and fashions indicate it is the Edinburgh of the early 1950s. Note the crowds enjoying the show at the old Ross Bandstand in West Princes Street Gardens and the tram stop in the centre of Princes Street, which is still paved in the stone setts that were a feature of the city.

wheep in case of a runaway. New routes quickly followed, but the innovative Edinburgh Northern Tramways Company had its eyes set on a powered cable system, and in 1888 the inaugural journey from Hanover Street to Goldenacre shoogled into existence. The power station and cable car depot was sited at Henderson Row, and by the end of 1900 almost all the 'animal-powered' vehicles had gone.

Like today, advertisers were quick to see the commercial advantage in a mobile billboard, and soon tram destinations were difficult to find among the hoardings for Bovril, Rising Sun floor polish, Suchard's Cocoa and Sanitas disinfectant. A number and colour system was introduced in 1907. A No 3 tram took the route from Abbeyhill to Ardmillan Terrace and was coloured blue, for example, a No 8 was Pilrig to Salisbury Place and always red. Edinburgh had a great affection for its trams and those chatty, friendly conductors — where are they now? — and after experiencing power by horse, cable, steam and electricity, it was a sad day when the last of them headed for their Shrubhill depot on November 16, 1956.

Was it the last? Edinburgh's vehicle-clogged streets and chronic parking problems have forced the city to consider again some form of light transport system for the future. It is not impossible that the tram will make its return in another guise, certainly with a different sound. It is the sound of the trams that lingers nostalgically through the years, indescribable perhaps for those who have never heard it, but was there ever greater boyhood delight than standing at the GPO at the east end of Princes Street, that throbbing tramcar junction, listening to the rattles, clanks, hisses, screeches, squeals, that delectable grinding-whomping-crunching sound and watching the flashes and sparks fly on a dark evening? Or would it be considered today environmental noise pollution and hounded?

Whatever insults were thrown at superannuated trams, they made a better job of transporting people around the city during rush hour than in today's constipated streets. Central Edinburgh is a car jungle of traffic clog, and hunting a parking place has now displaced the weather as the Capital's main topic of conversation. Cars — and their fumes — are one of the major environmental menaces of the Nineties and the ancient New Town is in the frontline of battle and losing. In most modern cities people live in the suburbs and travel to town to work. In Edinburgh, with its large New Town residential community, a major part of the suburbs is already in the heart of town. The rest of the suburbs and commuter traffic arrive in the morning to lay claim to the remaining parking spaces and become increasingly frustrated when they cannot find one. In summer they are joined by a host of visitors competing for the same places. The result is chaos. And anger. And lost business for a commercial community that depends on good business for its existence. And a poor image of Edinburgh for a city trying to attract even more tourists. And the heritage fabric of Georgian Edinburgh under stress. And disgruntled residents who cannot find parking for their own cars. And levels of carbon dioxide which at times reach unacceptable levels on Princes Street.

The ramifications for central Edinburgh if it is unable to solve its transport problems are far-reaching. The build-up of giant single-stop stores on the periphery of town because it is easier to park will change the face of Princes Street shopping unless there are improvements centrally. Why should people fight for a parking space in George Street through an assault course of red lights and traffic hazards when by driving a few miles to the superstore they can park free and with convenience? Princes Street must compete at that level and on the terms that customers want or decline into becoming a speciality shopping mall only. There are fewer parking places now than a decade ago at a time when there are more cars. In the future it will worsen because although cars will be smaller to conserve energy, there will be more per family, they will drive around Edinburgh and they will want to park side by side with the increased number of tourists.

If answers were simple, no doubt a solution would have been implemented long ago. Build more central car parks is one of them, but it is a short-term stopgap measure, and in the long run they are likely to suck larger and unacceptable vehicle volumes into the city. In a city of hills like Edinburgh more underground car parks seem obvious, but the cost of building them is prohibitive, we are told, and in the end they may be self-defeating anyway. So what solutions are being sought? Raising parking charges to price motorists out of central Edinburgh, the creation of park-and-ride systems that may ease problems in a small way but certainly not solve them, and the bully-boy introduction of the clamp, or car removal by the police appear to be the main tinkerings. The heavy stick approach is no substitute for a clear-cut traffic disposal policy.

There has been much circular talk for 30 years on Edinburgh's traffic problems, inquiries and research conducted and reports written on the subject, and still positive solutions seem as distant as ever. Perhaps the metro plan or some other kind of light-transport system will in the end be the way ahead and it has the merit of appearing to work in some Continental cities as well as being environmentally attractive. But it is expensive and the answers to how installation would be funded other than vaguely dumping it into the Government's lap are muddy and give little confidence that final decisions are even close. There is a perception that the politicians are complacent, that they are in no hurry because they do not have solutions that are politically or financially acceptable at present, so they are prepared to wait it out until someone else takes the lead or Edinburgh streets become so throttled and the public so outraged that money will magically be made available to hurl at the problem. Not only would such an approach be bad planning, it would also be bad politics. Such tactics are certainly not unknown and sometimes they can procure results but not without heartburn. Perhaps the politicians simply do not know which way to turn. No doubt they are as frustrated as everyone else, but if that is the case they should say so or finalise a plan with a timescale. It may even be that short-term measures are expedient to allow time to put long-term solutions in place. But in detail what are the long-term solutions for central Edinburgh? The problems are acute now, and now is when action is required.

The traffic build-up began in the 1950s, it was a feature of the Sixties when the notorious inner ring road plan was proposed that would have wreaked more damage to Edinburgh's heritage than German bombers could achieve during the war years, and the problems have been intensifying ever since. There were no difficulties with private cars during the war in Edinburgh because there were so few car-owners and petrol shortages put them off the road anyway. Even into the early Fifties you could almost choose your parking spot.

In comparison to other cities Edinburgh escaped the war lightly. The city endured it and lived daily the frontline conflict vicariously through wartime radio and the reports in Edinburgh's three daily newspapers at that time — *The Scotsman*, the *Evening Dispatch* and the *Evening News* (and later four with the launch of the *Scottish Daily Mail* in 1946, printed out of the old Tanfield offices in Canonmills). As in all great dramas, the recollections of those who lived through them are vivid and 50 years ago, when the Second World War raged, the memories of New Towners who made the best of it on their Home Front are rich in detail:

I REMEMBER almost everything that happened on that 1939 September Sunday when war was declared. Hibs had lost five goals at home to Albion Rovers on the Saturday and somehow I took it as an omen for bad news. The country was waiting beside the wireless to hear Neville Chamberlain's speech, but as a Royal Scot I was attending a church parade in St George's while the broadcast took place. Someone came in and whispered to our colonel, the colonel told the minister and the announcement for me that we were at war came from the pulpit. As I said to the lads afterwards, had Hibs won we might have had peace in our time after all!

I REMEMBER the big air raid shelters in Princes Street Gardens beside the Scott Monument. I used to think I would rather face the bombs than go down there because the Scott Monument may fall on top of us.

I REMEMBER joining that fine body of men — the Local Defence Volunteers based in The Edinburgh Academy in Henderson Row. I made good friends there and still meet up with some of them. Some of us were quite young and in reserved

The road is up on North Bridge again! This time it is to lay new cables into the post office. The year is 1952 and, yes, it is at the end of July, just in time to inconvenience Festival-goers. This is one of Edinburgh's busiest junctions, but there are still no signs of the massive revolution in personal transport. The tram is still king and the No 6 is on the Marchmont Circle route. A policeman on the lamp standard island prepares to direct the traffic in the absence of lights.

occupations, but we took the training seriously and I was quite a good shot with the old 303 Lee Enfield out at Hunter's Bog and we screamed with the best of them at bayonet charges. When we joined first we did our practice in civilian

181

Rush hour in Princes Street and it is quicker to walk . . . 'central Edinburgh has become a car jungle of traffic clog and hunting a parking place has almost displaced the weather as a topic of conversation. Cars — and their fumes — are one of the major environmental menaces in the 90s and the New Town is in the frontline of battle and losing'.

clothes with a khaki armband with LDV printed on it. Dad's Army came in for a lot of fun-poking, but if it had come to the bit we would have done an effective job.

I CAN REMEMBER as clear as day going up to Waverley Station with the rest of the children being evacuated from Canonmills School. My mother called me about 6 a.m. and made a terrible fuss. Just before I got onto the train the string came off my gasmask box and she had an awful job fixing it. She was almost in tears. I remember watching her get smaller and smaller as the train drew out of the station and it was only then I realised that I wouldn't be home that night. I sat down in my seat and grat.

I REMEMBER we were all given a banana as the children from the old Broughton School climbed on the special evacuees' train at Powderhall Station. We all had our gasmasks and a bag or suitcase and our names and addresses on labels tied to our coats. That banana was the last one I saw until the end of the war. We went over to Fife, but I was home again after three weeks. Had we known Edinburgh was to miss the blitz we probably wouldn't have gone in the first place.

THE BLACKOUT was a pain in the neck. We lived in Chester Street and what a job we had fitting our blackout frame to the windows. We'd heard all about how horrible the ARP wardens could be but the lad who came to tell us that he could see a chink of light outside was very pleasant. My mother promised that she'd see to it the next day, but something cropped up and it wasn't done. That's when the shouting started. It was a different warden the next night and, yes, he did shout those famous words at the top of his voice: 'Put out that light'. And it was no joke!

I REMEMBER I was expecting my Dad to arrive on leave any day. I heard these footsteps coming up the stair and assumed it was him. I pulled open the door and threw myself in to the arms of the postman.

THE WAR NEVER touched us really in Rothesay Place as I remember, but I was quite young then. My mother used to complain about the sugar rationing, but we had farming friends near Peebles and there were always plenty of eggs in the house. What I do remember is my Uncle Tom taking me down to see the land-mine damage to the David Kilpatrick's School in Leith. I was shocked. It was a terrible mess and I suppose I was a little frightened. For no real reason I began to cry.

I REMEMBER standing in Princes Street Gardens and watching the first aerial dogfight of the war over Edinburgh. German bombers over our city as bold as brass in broad daylight — it was impossible! Of course, it was all over quite quickly, and we didn't know if we were frightened or thrilled. I recollect there was a hoo-ha at the time because no sirens sounded.

AFTER the war it was a great time for dancing. Real dancing, not the dopey stuff the kids do today. They don't even hold on to the lasses these days. We used to go to the Ambassador Ballroom in Hamilton Place. It was the Al Jones band and his

Edinburgh at war and a Messerschmit 109, shot down over Kent, goes on display in Princes Street Gardens to launch the WVS Fighting Planes Fund. Lady Ruth Balfour, the first Scottish President of the WVS, is second from the right. The year is 1940 and air raid shelters are already in place in the shadow of the Scott Monument. The first aerial dog-fight of the war took place above the city, but Edinburgh was spared the bombardments endured by others.

singer, if I remember right, was Alexandra. The Princes Ballroom was in Princes Street, of course, and you could go in the afternoon or the evening. It was dearer in the evening but you got tea in the afternoon. The Balmoral Rooms were in Princes Street as well. I used to go to Fairley's with my mates on a Saturday night at the top of the Walk. It sounds daft now, but their resident band was called the New Rascals. Fairley's was called the Victoria Palais then and there were a lot of soldiers clomping about in army boots. It got a bit rough sometimes. The very opposite was MacDonald's Ballroom in Fettes Row. The manager wouldn't let you off with anything.

I WAS ONLY old enough to go to the pictures as the war ended. The cinema was the great attraction in those days. We lived in Hamilton Place and I used to go with my mother and Auntie Janet and there was a great choice of cinemas all around us. We used to walk to the Palace in Princes Street, the Grand and the Savoy at Stockbridge, the Playhouse at Greenside Place, Poole's Synod Hall and the Rutland was in Shandwick Place. All the big names were showing: Clark Gable, Spencer Tracey, Rita Hayworth, Tyrone Power, Ginger Rogers. I remember going to see Randolph Scott in *The Desperadoes* three times and I have been a fan of cowboy pictures ever since.

I'LL TELL YOU this about the war, the wireless was better than television today. Great Shows. Tommy Handley, Wilfred Pickles, Vic Oliver, Bebe Daniels and Ben Lyon. Laugh-a-minute stuff. And it was the age of the big bands like Geraldo, Mantovani, Billy Munn, Charles Enesco and his Sextet and there was Charles Smart on the organ and, of course, Billy Cotton, although his 'Waikey, waikey' theme didn't go down too well in Scotland Street. Too English. But the Carroll Lewis show was always good and I always listened to Henry Hall.

The war in Europe ended on Tuesday May 8, 1945 — VE Day — and the people took to the streets. It was anticipated, of course, and Princes Street Gardens had floodlights installed ready for a party as early as September, 1944. When the news of Germany's official surrender came, people simply rushed out and hugged each other. The bunting and flags were out, impromptu street parties were held all over the city. The city centre was mobbed by cheering, dancing, singing crowds that brought Princes Street traffic to a standstill. A Canadian Army sergeant had been deposited by his friends under a bush in Princes Street Gardens to sleep off the party spirit, which lay beside him in two almost empty bottles, and he too was cheered and cheered. Daisy Powders, the recommended potion to relieve headaches, were almost sold out. It was a time to laugh and cry, sing and shout, dance the night away, get drunk and pray, fall into melancholy with the not-so-good memories of those who were not coming back, or too crippled to be caught up in the joy, or friends or relatives who had been lost in the bombing. It was a time to be a little crazy and to thank God it was over.

Victory Day was June 8, 1946. It began with a riding of the marches for the first time in Edinburgh for 250 years to mark the occasion and it finished when the city's licensed premises had run out of supplies. The Lord Provost summed it up: 'You may well walk with your heads erect for you belong to a glorious country which has won great renown. You will always remember this day and keep in mind the price which has been paid so that you might live in gladness and peace.'

After the war the New Town was in a sad state like the rest of central Edinburgh. Necessary checking and repair work had not been easy, maintenance slipped, the fabric of the buildings was deteriorating fast, the Old Town was dying, some of the worst slums in Europe were at Greenside, St James Square was crumbling. The New Town was not on the same critical list as the Old Town, but generally it had the appearance of an exceedingly faded lady.

But with Europe in real devastation, rubble and dust, the thought of mere conservation in Edinburgh seemed hardly even a priority. Some traditional New Town families envisaged the end of what had once been a lifestyle of grandeur in beautiful and historic surroundings and moved to the Grange, Morningside, Murrayfield or out of town entirely. Decay and neglect had brought the Old Town to the brink of a heritage disaster, and to the undying credit of Edinburgh it was decided that if it was going to be restored — and such a national heritage must be preserved — then the task should be implemented with distinction. The efforts in the Old Town have resulted in some of the finest conservation work anywhere, although there are notable exceptions like the tasteless Regional Council offices, which remain a jarring note in a highly sensitive historical area and must lay claim to being on Prince Charles's list of British architectural carbuncles. The restoration of Chessel's Court and White Horse Close were early triumphs and the process continues and widens into the Grassmarket and the South Side, the latest refurbishment developments.

Over in the New Town life carried on uneasily for those who cared about preservation as they watched the telltale signs of fabric deterioration. 'Doing something about the New Town' became a general informal talking point among architects, planners, residents and councillors, but it was not until the Scottish Civic Trust was created in May of 1967 with its brief to stimulate interest in the environment that the problems were given focus. Assessing the extent of those New Town problems was the first important step, then a major conference was held in June 1970 organised by the Scottish Civic Trust, the Edinburgh Architectural Association and the Civic Trust of London, chaired by architect Sir Robert Matthew, and the impetus was launched. Edinburgh may be justifiably criticised at times for its slowness to react, its talent to procrastinate, its genius for splintering into opposing factions to frustrate, but whatever its record in other areas, once it was finally decided that the moment for New Town action had arrived and the financial grants were in place, it was carried out with commendable professionalism.

What was impressive about that 1970 conference was that it mobilised the significant figures in architecture and conservation both nationally and internationally. A united Edinburgh behind a common cause is a formidable force because it can involve people at the highest level of influence. The Count Sforza, of the Council of Europe, was there and spoke with affection of a city which he had never previously visited but which, like most Europeans, he had always regarded as one of Europe's outstanding examples of culture and beauty. And suddenly Edinburgh was once more being projected onto the European stage, discussed in comparable terms with Venice, Rome and Paris and other great European capitals. It was as if all those aspirations presented in 'The Proposals' of 1752 and Lord Provost George Drummond's arguments to persuade Edinburgh to leap the Nor' Loch and build the New Town were echoing down two centuries as speaker after speaker adopted them again to argue the need now to preserve it. The conference achieved three important results: the commitment to preserve the New Town was established, Georgian Edinburgh as an architectural treasure was recognised, and it sparked a zeal and a will and an understanding of the meaning of heritage that has continued.

The success of the initiatives and action that followed has been well documented. What is perhaps not generally appreciated is the scale of the success. It is an enormous ongoing project, one of the biggest of its kind in the world. It has taken a cast of thousands over the years from official bodies, government departments, individual experts, architects, councillors, civil servants, conservation groups, amenity and residents' associations, the business community, and senior and local politicians from Scottish Secretaries of State downwards working in partnership in infinite detail.

The saving of the New Town has been supported by residents with highly organised and motivated street associations, some of whom hardly knew an astragal from their elbow in the early days, but now are knowledgeable and dedicated conservationists. A New Town Conservation Committee was formed and full-time director Desmond Hodges and his staff at 13A Dundas Street are pleased and able to help and advise on a range of problems, some of them highly technical. They carry out inspection work and administer the generous grants from the Scottish Office and Edinburgh District Council which have made the whole enterprise possible. Their work, of course, will never be completed. Parts of the New Town are still in need of repair, the northern edge is undergoing major attention, and it is now the turn of St Stephen Street and its surrounds to be transformed to the surprise of passers-by who see the basement-to-top-floor height and dignity of the old flats in a new light. The preservation of the New Town must essentially be a continuing process.

Even in the long ago Edinburgh's environmental consciousness was ready to assert itself. One of the biggest green battles in the city took place in the 19th century when the quarrying of Salisbury Crags began to disfigure the face of Arthur's Seat to provide 'calsey staines' for paving the New Town's streets. Those cliffs above the Radical Road did not achieve that shape on their own account, and a major legal battle was fought to have the quarrying stopped before the natural beauty of our extinct volcano was irretrievably scarred. The

The New Town is one of the largest and almost pristine 'Georgian' developments in the world. It is Edinburgh's heritage. But the wear and tear of two centuries — as well as neglect — has left its mark and even cost the city the loss of St James Square. In an age when 'green' issues are only now being better understood, Edinburgh has been one of the leaders in the conservation battle for more than two decades. The conservation of the New Town, one of the biggest projects of its kind in the world, has been an enormous success story. The following sequence of photographs traces some of that success.

ABOVE — the view from the east side of St Stephen Street shows Nos. 20 to 60 in a state of substantial disrepair.

OPPOSITE — the transformation that has generated new life and character for the street.

case went to the House of Lords and the quarrying was finally stopped in 1831. Environmental mistakes are not new; sometimes they are innocently made, sometimes for expediency or profit, but people are more alert to them than ever before. Such is the amount of development in Edinburgh at the present time, however, with new plans and strategies following in such rapidity that the public finds it difficult to take a perspective and therefore, hopefully, exert some control. New plans and ideas must never run ahead of public understanding. In that direction lie mistakes and regrets and Edinburgh has had enough of these in the past.

Already the biggest building programme since the making of the New Town is planned for Edinburgh's western extremity around the Maybury across 180 acres, a shopping complex worth £450 million, offering 20,000 jobs and 7000 car parking places, and those who believe Princes Street and George Street will be unaffected are ostriches. In the future wheels will speak, range of shopping with convenience, quality and pleasure and ease of car parking will decide where people go. Commercial central Edinburgh will be challenged to its foundations to rediscover itself to meet shoppers' needs. If it fails to do so it will increasingly become residential again — two centuries come full cycle — or the biggest tourists' gift emporium in the world. And not too many of the existing traders can live in that scenario.

The future of Princes Street, of course, certainly need not be in that direction. So much can be done to effect improvements. It may mean a radical approach, new ideas and the will to see them through, but encouragingly many even now are under consideration. Even suggestions from the Sixties like a covered walkway the length of Princes Street are being dusted down, although the idea of a two-way moving pavement is perhaps still too futuristic. Some imaginative accommodation can surely be reached over parking. Private car parks are not always full, meter parking could sensibly be increased, more short-stay areas created, which would mean selected hiked charges, but with the Maybury project in mind, somehow access for shoppers has to be made easier in the centre of the city. The improvement of public transport is fundamental. Better packaging of the central area could also increase its attraction: redesigned street furniture, flower displays, groupings of specialist interests like books or antiques or paintings identified with particular streets, which could still be cleaner, undercover activities like street theatre and exhibitions. Some are hoary suggestions and have been around a long time, but they are being seriously appraised because survival demands it and central Edinburgh must compete. Perhaps at last Princes Street will even put to better use that mile-long top-of-shop storage space that has hung unproductively above it for years. Given access to private flats, there would be a stampede to own property with such a vista of Castle and Royal Mile on one side and the Forth and Fife panorama out of the back window. It may mean altering the architecture at the rear, but that proposition is also there to be considered.

Of course, trying to build or create something new in central Edinburgh is like a motorcyclist from the Tattoo leaping through his hoop of fire. The conservation bodies see to that. Yet if they momentarily relaxed their nit-picking, planning disasters would ruin Edinburgh's face. In fact, in spite of their attention, it is sad to see so many hopeful plans fall short of their potential on implementation. The Mound Square, for example, is a travesty of what was originally envisaged. And those who remember the nomadic movements of the

The scaffolding goes up on Carlton Street to reinstate the balustrade, rebuild the chimneys and clean the stone. The cost of this refurbishment was around £320,000.

The scaffolding comes down to unveil Carlton Street's splendid new old face on Nos. 3 to 13. Not only has the future of the street been assured, but once more it is turned into an attractive and desirable property.

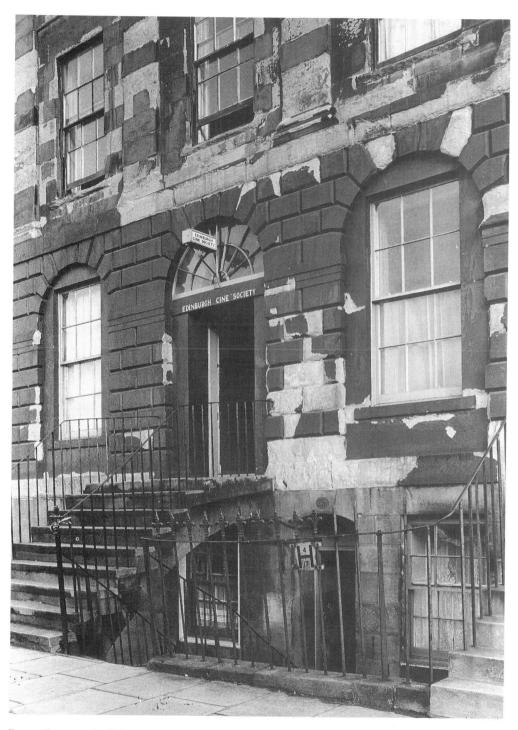

Fettes Row was built between 1819 and 1828, but the years began to take their toll. Even the once-smart railings were loosening and falling masonry became a hazard. Fettes Row was the first comprehensive conservation project in the New Town and the start of a remarkable success story.

Life Association of Scotland from its David Rhind magnificence on Princes Street by way of a marbled filing cabinet in George Street to its present site at the bottom of Dundas Street with its stringy, apologetic stone colonnades like stacked toilet rolls must wonder at its courage to stay in the New Town rather than fade more easily into the periphery. How entirely unfair! The LAS effort has been courageous and expensive and offers one of the best-designed interiors in the city and an exterior which is an imaginative link with the past but in modern architectural idiom. It is no mere slavish recreation of a glorious Georgian past, which is neither feasible nor desirable, but a demonstration of genuine aspiration to marry past and future, which is more than some of its immediate neighbours have attempted. Or does it? Take your pick! It certainly isn't everyone's cup of tea. But both camps have their supporters. Perhaps there is no answer to the kind of questions such opposing arguments present. Maybe it is just that the LAS building is different. One side wants to justify it, the other fear loss of quality long term as more and more of its close relatives are erected, and in a city of traditionalists, conservative by nature, change is almost always anticipated negatively.

For those who follow Edinburgh dilemmas, the greening of the Waverley valley across the unloved glass roof of the station will give particular satisfaction. The valley from Waverley through Princes Street Gardens to the Caledonian Hotel in the east, with the Old Town skyline above facing Princes Street, is Edinburgh's greatest natural asset. A step wrong here and, as was pointed out by a prominent planning authority more than 20 years ago, the result will be a 'coffin in the valley'. Here the whole character of Scotland's capital is set, imparting a quality that is beyond price. Already ideas for alterations and 'improvements' for this sensitive area are being discussed as British Rail finalise their requirements for electrification and a link with the Channel Tunnel. A brainstorming competition trawling for inspiration resulted in some excellent suggestions, as well as flights of fancy and also a hardening of parameters as the free flow of creative thought swept along the Waverley line. Burying the railway out of sight, conversely making it an above-ground celebration as behoves a great railway city, restoring the Nor' Loch so that the wonders of the skyline above can be reflected below, moving the main body of the station to Haymarket, unlocking new vistas, the broad brush-stroke of creating an island of focus relating to the steeples of West End churches and the enfolding curve of the Royal Mile,

OPPOSITE

Before the conservation programme the perspective of Fettes Row Nos. 22 and 23 was a patchwork of dilapidation and decay. Yet the classic lines are still obvious, the elegant fanlights still in place. Without restoration its days are limited before the demolishers move in.

Let work commence . . . a fretwork of scaffolding hides the activity, but the symbol of the New Town's Conservation Committee informs passers-by that restoration is in progress. St Stephen's Church is in the background.

Transformation again . . . the operation has been a huge success. It is 1975 and this part of Heriot Row is restored and returned to its former state. This was the first project, but many more have followed.

Such success deserves recognition and Queen Elizabeth, the Queen Mother, was pleased to visit Nos. 23 and 24 Fettes Row to give it royal acknowledgement as well as encouragement for the efforts ahead. The conservation of the New Town has been a team effort from the start between central government, local authority, the various conservation groups and the residents themselves. Many residents have become conservation zealots, highly-organised and alert to look after the New Town's best interests.

developing Princes Street Gardens with an amphitheatre which could mean permanent transposal from the Castle Esplanade for the Military Tattoo, further enclosing the valley, opening it up, perhaps more shops, some office space, the creation of Market Street as an arts centre, building above Princes Street, which would require an Act of Parliament, yet another new hotel, perhaps a further conference centre. They were only suggestions. But something will happen, sooner or later changes will be forced on this central jewel that remains a site of international importance, just as inevitably as change is sweeping throughout the city.

How exciting! And thought-provoking! And worrying! What an opportunity for distinction — or for a catastrophe! Or will it all be played too safely and blandness result?

When there is a surfeit of choice and advice and the road to take is unclear or bumpy, it does no harm to recall how the New Town was built, how George Drummond got things moving against all the odds, how James Craig and Robert Adam put their stamp on it for ever, how in their separate ways they issued a challenge to those who would follow to do better if they could. Edinburgh's impetus and direction may have been lost many times since those days, but hopefully the same instincts are alive and well since Adam and Playfair and William Burn and Gillespie Graham and Bryce, Rhind, Anderson, Lorimer, Lissels, Elliot, Pugin, Stark and the many other rich talents who helped to create the New Town with pride.

Today Edinburgh is embarking on perhaps its biggest building programme this century. Not as a single scheme or building, but right across the face of the entire city new homes, office blocks, hotels, an enormous hypermarket, public and private developments of all kinds, some of them joint enterprises, are being built or planned and the process will continue throughout the Nineties. Obviously they will not be created in the same style and manner and material as was used by the old masters, and that is understood, but modern planning and architecture at its best can also be exciting and enduring. What is important is that what can be conserved of the old order is left for posterity and the new Edinburgh adventure is aimed at creating with quality and style and excellence at its core a city that truly and sensitively reflects the Edinburgh of the past. That is most important. Edinburgh isn't just any city, and that challenge echoing from the New Town after 200 years is waiting to be picked up.

BIBLIOGRAPHY

Arnot, Hugo, *History of Edinburgh* (1779)

Barclay, J. B., *Edinburgh from Earliest Times to the Present Day*

Birrell, J. F., *An Edinburgh Alphabet*

Books of the Old Edinburgh Club

Catford, E. F., *Edinburgh — the Story of a City*

Chambers, Robert, *Traditions of Edinburgh*

Cockburn, Lord, *Memorials of his Time*

Crossland, J. Brian, *Victorian Edinburgh*

Daiches, David, *Edinburgh*

Edinburgh Architectural Association, *Edinburgh — An Architectural Guide*

Grant, James, *Old and New Edinburgh*

Lindsay, Ian G., *Georgian Edinburgh*

Lockhart, J. G., *Memoirs of Sir Walter Scott*

Maitland, W., *History of Edinburgh*

McLaren, Moray, *The capital of Scotland, Stevenson and Edinburgh*

Nimmo, Ian, *Portrait of Edinburgh, Scotland at War*

Royle, Trevor, *Precipitous City*

Rankin, Nicholas, *Dead Man's Chest — Travels after Robert Louis Stevenson*

Scott-Moncrieff, George, *Edinburgh*

Sinclair, Sir John (Ed), *The Statistical account of Scotland*, vol. VI, Edinburgh

Smout, T. C., *A Century of the Scottish People 1830–1950*

Stevenson, R. L., *Edinburgh — Picturesque Notes*

Youngston, A. J., *The Making of Classical Edinburgh*

INDEX

201